D0374989

WHERE THE SILENCE RINGS

edited and with an introduction by
WAYNE GRADY

A LITERARY COMPANION
to MOUNTAINS

WHERE
THE SILENCE
RINGS

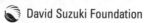 David Suzuki Foundation

GREYSTONE BOOKS
Douglas & McIntyre Publishing Group
VANCOUVER/TORONTO/BERKELEY

Greystone Books
A division of Douglas & McIntyre Ltd.
2323 Quebec Street, Suite 201
Vancouver, BC, Canada v5T 4S7
www.greystonebooks.com

David Suzuki Foundation
219–2211 West 4th Avenue
Vancouver, BC, Canada v6K 4S2

Library and Archives Canada Cataloguing in Publication
Where the silence rings : a literary companion to
mountains / edited and with an introduction by Wayne Grady.
Co-published by the David Suzuki Foundation.

ISBN 978-1-55365-243-4

1. Mountains—Literary collections. 1. Grady, Wayne 11. David Suzuki Foundation
PN6071.M738W48 2007   808.84'932143   C2007-900416-4

Cover and text design by Peter Cocking
Cover images © Veer Incorporated
Printed and bound in Canada by Friesens
Printed on acid-free paper that is forest friendly
(100% post-consumer recycled paper) and has been processed chlorine free.
Distributed in the U.S. by Publishers Group West

We gratefully acknowledge the financial support of the Canada Council for the Arts,
the British Columbia Arts Council, and the Government of Canada through the Book
Publishing Industry Development Program (BPIDP) for our publishing activities.

CONTENTS

INTRODUCTION

HOMO SAPIENS is a grasslands species: our ancestral home is the vast savannas of subequatorial Africa, and our preferred vista is still an expanse of flat prairie dotted with a few trees and the occasional river. So whence our undeniable fascination with mountains?

Clearly the ancients venerated mountains and associated them with the gods. The Greek deities lived on Mount Olympus, a 9,000-foot peak in northeastern Greece; Greek poets lauded the somewhat lower (8,000-foot) Mount Parnassus, sacred to the Muses: directives for living long and prosperous lives came from both peaks. In Christian literature, the Ark was stranded on Mount Ararat, Moses received the Ten Commandments on Mount Sinai, the great temple of Jerusalem was built on Mount Zion, and Jesus preached his most important sermon on the Mount of Olives. As well, "sacred mountains and pilgrimages to them is a deeply established feature of the popular religions of Asia," writes Gary Snyder in *The Practice of the Wild*. "There are hundreds of famous Daoist and Buddhist peaks in China and similar Buddhist and Shinto-associated mountains in Japan." The lure may be because mountains are often associated with water, as Carl Jung suggests in the excerpt from *Memories, Dreams, Reflections* included in these pages. Snyder mentions the thirteenth-century Japanese Dogen Kigen and his work, "Mountains and Waters Sutra," in which the Dogen writes: "Because mountains and waters have been active since before the eon of emptiness, they are alive at this moment."

This "active-ness" accounts in part for mountains' irresistible attraction: in geological terms, as we now know, mountains are often literally active, the most recent parts of Earth to have been created, the last bits to have been touched by the gods, and because of their height the closest we can come to heaven on Earth. Mountains almost always form at the edges of continents, where tectonic plates collide and fold, dividing (and protecting) the plains from the incursive oceans, and providing good views of both.

But the fact that mountains play such a significant role in human religions suggests a deeper element to their attraction. Driving west across the continent recently, I entered the Rocky Mountains after several days of crossing the hot, populous prairies, and there was no denying the lift that the mountains gave to my spirits. I wanted to stop and climb, to lose myself in the enclosing cliffs, follow cascading streams up into misted, secluded valleys. After days of being able to see to the distant, unreachable horizon, in the mountains I wanted to walk to see what lay behind the confining ridge. More ridges, I suspected, and more ridges after that: an endless series of sacred, sheltering sites that were "alive at this moment."

There are, of course, other factors. In the past 35,000 years or so, we humans have expanded our range beyond the grasslands of Africa into every climatic zone the Earth has to offer, and to do that we had to risk crossing mountains. We are, or at least we became, a risk-taking species—a characteristic that nowadays finds outlet in such extreme sports as mountain climbing. Mountains are wild places where the risks are real and immediate, and the consequences of failure, one missed step, a split-second of inattention, are sudden and irrevocable—as countless mountaineers know from experience, including Edward Whymper, the nineteenth-century Alpinist whose account of his team's ascent of the Matterhorn opens this collection. Tragedy at great heights doesn't deter us from continuing to climb mountains, any more than tragedy on the stage deters us from returning to the theatre. As W.H. Auden and Christopher Isherwood observed in their play about mountain climbing, *The Ascent of F6*, "there's more than a mountain at stake."

The Dogen Kigen's assertion that mountains and waters are alive reflects an ancient belief that all nature was animated and acted according to an unknowable and unpredictable willfulness that was usually at odds with order-imposing humankind. Mountains were the terrible haunts of ogres, monsters, faeries and goblins, creatures that occupied a twilight zone between human and wild. Thus Shakespeare's Gonzalo, in *The Tempest*, speaks of "mountayneers dew-lapt like bulls." But during the Age of Science, which began shortly after Shakespeare's life-time, nature came to be seen as operating according to physical laws that are knowable. Mountains became objects of interest for a whole new set of reasons: they were demonstrations of the powerful effects of the forces of nature. They now exercised upon the human imagination what the English essayist Joseph Addison, in describing the Alps near Geneva, referred to as "an agreeable kind of horror"—horrible because they reminded us of our own insignificance in the face of natural forces, and agreeable because they put us in touch with traces of those forces as they acted in us. According to William Robert Irwin, editor of *Challenge: An Anthology of the Literature of Mountain-eering* (1950), this changing view of mountains—from terror to be avoided to terror to be pursued—resulted in mountains act-ing "as stimulants to the imagination," specifically the Roman-tic imagination.

The Swiss Alps in particular became the playground of Europe, with poets like Wordsworth, Byron, and Shelley clam-bering over their lower reaches, and more serious-minded but no less romantic persons—Whymper, Sir Leslie Stephen, John Buchan—also finding in mountains the kind of aesthetic as well as physical catalysts that connected them to nature. Jonathan Raban, in *Passage to Juneau*, addresses this fascination with mountaineering, linking it to accounts of explorations pour-ing into England from such far-off, romantic terrae incogni-tae as Australia and the Pacific Northwest. "By the 1810s," he writes, "when the Alps and the Lake District were beginning to swarm with hikers, there was a hunger for some landscape more unvisited, wild, and sublime than Europe could supply. Extreme experiences—the peaks and chasms of love and death, which were at the heart of the Romantic movement in writing and painting—required a corresponding extremity, and loneliness, in nature." Painter, writer, and mountain climber Belmore Browne, whose attempt to reach the summit of Alaska's Mount McKinley (now known as Denali) is reproduced here, is a case in point, and the Canadian poet Earle Birney, whose poem "David" is also included, is a modern inheritor of that romantic association with danger, death, and inspiration.

Much of the literature of mountains has to do with science and natural history, the quest to understand those physical laws that govern all natural phenomena, from mountains to amoebae. John Muir, the indefatigable champion of the California wilderness, spent a wintry night on Mount Shasta partly in order to know more intimately how its natural inhabitants managed it. Peter Matthiessen and Jamaica Kincaid were both drawn to the Himalayas, the former in search of the rare, nearly mythical snow leopard, the latter as a collector of seeds for her Vermont garden.

As Irwin also remarks, "from the first, climbing has attracted persons of high intellectual and artistic capacity." I never did stop my car as I drove through the Rockies, never walked off into the wilderness to see what was beyond the nearest range, but we as readers—armchair climbers, most of us—are the beneficiaries of that curious capacity.

THE FIRST ASCENT
OF THE MATTERHORN

EDWARD WHYMPER

Whymper began with a passion for Arctic exploration, but when, in 1860, he was sent to Switzerland to do engravings for a book on the Alps, he switched his compass to mountaineering. He was the first to reach the summit of such legendary peaks as Mont Pelvoux, the Pointe des Ecrins, the Grand Cornier, and the Aiguille Verte. He attempted the Matterhorn seven times before finally reaching its peak in 1865, with seven other experienced climbers: Swiss guides Michel Croz, Peter Taugwalder and his two sons, Lord Francis Douglas, the Reverend Charles Hudson, and Hudson's friend, identified only as Mr. Hadow. The tragic story of that expedition, excerpted here from Whymper's book *Scrambles Amongst the Alps in the Years 1860–1869* (1871), is one of the classics of mountain literature.

. . .

WE STARTED FROM Zermatt on the 13th of July 1865, at half-past 5, on a brilliant and perfectly cloudless morning. We were eight in number—Croz, old Peter and his two sons, Lord F.

12

Douglas, Hadow, Hudson, and I. To ensure steady motion, one tourist and one native walked together. The youngest Taugwalder fell to my share, and the lad marched well, proud to be on the expedition, and happy to shew his powers. The winebags also fell to my lot to carry, and throughout the day, after each drink, I replenished them secretly with water, so that at the next halt they were found fuller than before! This was considered a good omen, and little short of miraculous.

On the first day we did not intend to ascend to any great height, and we mounted, accordingly, very leisurely; picked up the things which were left in the chapel at the Schwarzsee at 8:20, and proceeded thence along the ridge connecting the Hörnli with the Matterhorn. At half-past 11 we arrived at the base of the actual peak; then quitted the ridge, and clambered round some ledges, on to the eastern face. We were now fairly upon the mountain, and were astonished to find that places which from the Riffel, or even from the Furggengletscher, looked entirely impracticable, were so easy that we could *run about*.

Before twelve o'clock we had found a good position for the tent, at a height of 11,000 feet. Thus far the guides did not once go to the front. Hudson or I led, and when any cutting was required we did it ourselves. This was done to spare the guides, and to shew them that we were in earnest. Croz and young Peter went on to see what was above, in order to save time on the following morning. They cut across the heads of the snow-slopes which descended towards the Furggengletscher, and disappeared round a corner; but shortly afterwards we saw them high up on the face, moving quickly. We others made a solid platform for the tent in a well-protected spot, and then watched eagerly for the return of the men. The stones which they upset told us that they were very high, and we supposed that the way must be easy. At length, just before 3 PM, we saw them coming down, evidently much excited. "What are they saying, Peter?" "Gentlemen, they say it is no good." But when they came near we heard a different story. "Nothing but what was good; not a difficulty, not a single difficulty! We could have gone to the summit and returned to-day easily!"

We passed the remaining hours of daylight—some basking in the sunshine, some sketching or collecting; and when the sun went down, giving, as it departed, a glorious promise for the morrow, we returned to the tent to arrange for the night. Hudson made tea, I coffee, and we then retired each one to his blanket bag; the Taugwalders, Lord Francis Douglas, and myself, occupying the tent, the others remaining, by preference, outside. Long after dusk the cliffs above echoed with our laughter and with the songs of the guides, for we were happy that night in camp, and feared no evil.

We assembled together outside the tent before dawn on the morning of the 14th, and started directly it was light enough to move. Young Peter came on with us as a guide, and his brother returned to Zermatt. We followed the route which had been taken on the previous day, and in a few minutes turned the rib which had intercepted the view of the eastern face from our tent platform. The whole of this great slope was now revealed, rising for 3,000 feet like a huge natural staircase. Some parts were more, and others were less, easy; but we were not once brought to a halt by any serious impediment, for when an obstruction was met in front it could always be turned to the right or to the left. For the greater part of the way there was, indeed, no occasion for the rope, and sometimes Hudson led, sometimes myself. At 6:20 we had attained a height of 12,800 feet, and halted for half an hour; we then continued the ascent without a break until 9:55, when we stopped for fifty minutes, at a height of 14,000 feet. Twice we struck the N.E. ridge and followed it for some little distance—to no advantage, for it was usually more rotten and steep, and always more difficult than the face. Still, we kept near to it, lest stones perchance might fall.

We had now arrived at the foot of that part which, from the Riffelberg or from Zermatt, seems perpendicular or overhanging, and could no longer continue upon the eastern side. For a little distance we ascended by snow upon the arête—that is, the ridge—descending towards Zermatt, and then, by common consent, turned over to the right, or to the northern side. Before doing so, we made a change in the order of ascent. Croz went first, I followed, Hudson came third; Hadow and old Peter were last.

"Now," said Croz, as he led off, "now for something altogether different."

The work became difficult and required caution. In some places there was little to hold, and it was desirable that those should be in front who were least likely to slip. The general slope of the mountain at this part was *less* than 40°, and snow had accumulated in, and had filled up, the interstices of the rock-face, leaving only occasional fragments projecting here and there. These were at times covered with a thin film of ice, produced from the melting and refreezing of the snow. It was the counterpart, on a small scale, of the upper 700 feet of the Pointe des Ecrins—only there was this material difference; the face of the Ecrins was about, or exceeded, an angle of 50°, and the Matterhorn face was less than 40°. It was a place over which any fair mountaineer might pass in safety, and Mr. Hudson ascended this part, and, as far as I know, the entire mountain, without having the slightest assistance rendered to him upon any occasion. Sometimes, after I had taken a hand from Croz, or received a pull, I turned to offer the same to Hudson; but he invariably declined, saying it was not necessary. Mr. Hadow, however, was not accustomed to this kind of work, and required continual assistance. It is only fair to say that the difficulty which he found at this part arose simply and entirely from want of experience.

This solitary difficult part was of no great extent. We bore away over it at first, nearly horizontally, for a distance of about 400 feet; then ascended directly towards the summit for about 60 feet; and then doubled back to the ridge which descends towards Zermatt. A long stride round a rather awkward corner brought us to snow once more. The last doubt vanished! The Matterhorn was ours! Nothing but 200 feet of easy snow remained to be surmounted!

You must now carry your thoughts back to the seven Italians who started from Breuil on the 11th of July. Four days had passed since their departure, and we were tormented with anxiety lest they should arrive on the top before us. All the way up we had talked of them, and many false alarms of "men on the summit" had been raised. The higher we rose, the more intense became the excitement. What if we should be beaten at the last moment? The slope eased off, at length we could be detached, and Croz and I, dashing away, ran a neck-and-neck race, which ended in a dead heat. At 1:40 PM the world was at our feet, and the Matterhorn was conquered. Hurrah! Not a footstep could be seen.

It was not yet certain that we had not been beaten. The summit of the Matterhorn was formed of a rudely level ridge, about 350 feet long, and the Italians might have been at its farther extremity. I hastened to the southern end, scanning the snow right and left eagerly. Hurrah! again; it was untrodden. "Where were the men?" I peered over the cliff, half doubting, half expectant, and saw them immediately—mere dots on the ridge, at an immense distance below. Up went my arms and my hat. "Croz! Croz!! come here!" "Where are they, Monsieur?" "There, don't you see them, down there?" "Ah! the *coquins*, they are low down." "Croz, we must make those fellows hear us." We yelled until we were hoarse. The Italians seemed to regard us—we could not be certain. "Croz, we *must* make them hear us; they *shall* hear us!" I seized a block of rock and hurled it down, and called upon my companion, in the name of friendship, to do the same. We drove our sticks in, and prized away the crags, and soon a torrent of stones poured down the cliffs. There was no mistake about it this time. The Italians turned and fled...

The others had arrived, so we went back to the northern end of the ridge. Croz now took a tent-pole and planted it in the highest snow. "Yes," we said, "there is the flag-staff, but where is the flag?" "Here it is," he answered, pulling off his blouse and fixing it to the stick. It made a poor flag, and there was no wind to float it out, yet it was seen all around. They saw it at Zermatt—at the Riffel—in the Val Tournache. At Breuil, the watchers cried, "Victory is ours!" They raised 'bravos' for Carrel, and 'vivas' for Italy, and hastened to put themselves *en fête*. On the morrow they were undeceived. "All was changed; the explorers returned sad—cast down—disheartened—confounded—gloomy." "It is true," said the men. "We saw them ourselves—they hurled stones at us! The old traditions *are* true—there are spirits on the top of the Matterhorn!"

We returned to the southern edge of the ridge to build a cairn, and then paid homage to the view. The day was one of those superlatively calm and clear ones which usually precede bad weather. The atmosphere was perfectly still, and free from all clouds or vapours. Mountains fifty—nay a hundred—miles off, looked sharp and near. All their details—ridge and crag, snow and glacier—stood out with faultless definition. Pleasant thoughts of happy days in bygone years came up unbidden, as we recognised the old, familiar forms. All was revealed—not one of the principal peaks of the Alps was hidden. I see them clearly now—the great inner circles of giants, backed by the ranges, chains, and *massifs*. First came the Dent Blanche, hoary and grand; the Gabelhorn and pointed Rothhorn; and then the peerless Weisshorn: the towering Mischabelhörner, flanked by the Allaleinhorn, Strahlhorn, and Rimpfischhorn; then Monte Rosa—with its many Spitzes—the Lyskamm and the Breithorn. Behind were the Bernese Oberland, governed by the Finsteraar-horn; the Simplon and St. Gothard groups; the Disgrazia and the Orteler. Towards the south we looked down to Chivasso on the plain of Piedmont, and far beyond. The Viso—one hundred miles away—seemed close upon us; the Maritime Alps—one hundred and thirty miles distant—were free from haze. Then came my first love—the Pelvoux; the Ecrins and the Meije; the clusters of the Graians; and lastly, in the west, glowing in full sunlight, rose the monarch of all—Mont Blanc. Ten thousand feet beneath us were the green fields of Zermatt, dotted with châlets, from which blue smoke rose lazily. Eight thousand feet below, on the other side, were the pastures of Breuil. There were forests black and gloomy, and meadows bright and lively; bounding waterfalls and tranquil lakes; fertile lands and savage wastes; sunny plains and frigid *plateaux*. There were the most rugged forms, and the most graceful outlines—bold, perpen-dicular cliffs, and gentle, undulating slopes; rocky mountains and snowy mountains, sombre and solemn, or glittering and white, with walls—turrets—pinnacles—pyramids—domes—cones—and spires! There was every combination that the world can give, and every contrast that the heart could desire.

We remained on the summit for one hour—

"One crowded hour of glorious life."

It passed away too quickly, and we began to prepare for the descent.

THE DESCENT

Hudson and I again consulted as to the best and safest arrangement of the party. We agreed that it would be best for Croz to go first, and Hadow second; Hudson, who was almost equal to a born mountaineer in sureness of foot, wished to be third; Lord Francis Douglas was placed next, and old Peter, the strongest of the remainder, after him. I suggested to Hudson that we should attach a rope to the rocks on our arrival at the difficult bit, and hold it as we descended, as an additional protection. He approved the idea, but it was not definitely settled that it should be done. The party was being arranged in the above order whilst I was sketching the summit, and they had finished, and were waiting for me to be tied in line, when some one remembered that our names had not been left in a bottle. They requested me to write them down, and moved off while it was being done.

A few minutes afterwards I tied myself to young Peter, ran down after the others, and caught them just as they were commencing the descent of the difficult part. Great care was being taken. Only one man was moving at a time; when he was firmly planted the next advanced, and so on. They had not, however, attached the additional rope to rocks, and nothing was said about it. The suggestion was not made for my own sake, and I am not sure that it even occurred to me again. For some little distance we two followed the others, detached from them, and should have continued so had not Lord Francis Douglas asked me, about 3 PM, to tie on to old Peter, as he feared, he said, that Taugwalder would not be able to hold his ground if a slip occurred.

A few minutes later, a sharp-eyed lad ran into the Monte Rosa hotel, to Seiler, saying that he had seen an avalanche fall from the summit of the Matterhorn on to the Matterhorn-gletscher. The boy was reproved for telling idle stores; he was right, nevertheless, and this was what he saw.

Michel Croz had laid aside his axe, and in order to give Mr. Hadow greater security, was absolutely taking hold of his legs, and putting his feet, one by one, into their proper positions. So far as I know, no one was actually descending. I cannot speak with certainty, because the two leading men were partially hidden from my sight by an intervening mass of rock, but it is my belief, from the movements of their shoulders, that Croz, having done as I have said, was in the act of turning round, to go down a step or two himself; at this moment Mr. Hadow slipped, fell against him, and knocked him over. I heard one startled exclamation from Croz, then saw him and Mr. Hadow flying downwards; in another moment Hudson was dragged from his steps, and Lord F. Douglas immediately after him.

All this was the work of a moment. Immediately we heard Croz's exclamation, old Peter and I planted ourselves as firmly as the rocks would permit and held on as tightly as possible. There was no time to change our position. The rope was taut between us, and the jerk came on us both as on one man. We held; but the rope broke midway between Taugwalder and Lord Francis Douglas. For a few seconds we saw our unfortunate companions sliding downwards on their backs, and spreading out their hands, endeavouring to save themselves. They passed from our sight uninjured, disappeared one by one, and fell from precipice to precipice on to the Matterhorngletscher below, a distance of nearly 4,000 feet in height. From the moment the rope broke it was impossible to help them. . .

For more than two hours afterwards I thought almost every moment that the next would be my last; for the Taugwalders, utterly unnerved, were not only incapable of giving assistance, but were in such a state that a slip might have been expected from them at any moment. After a time we were able to do that which should have been done at first, and fixed rope to firm rocks, in addition to being tied together. The ropes were cut from time to time, and were left behind. Even with their assurance the men were afraid to proceed, and several times old Peter turned with ashy face and faltering limbs, and said, with terrible emphasis, "*I cannot!*"

About 6 PM we arrived at the snow upon the ridge descending towards Zermatt, and all peril was over. We frequently looked, but in vain, for traces of our unfortunate companions; we bent over the ridge and cried to them, but no sound returned. Convinced at last that they were neither within sight nor hearing, we ceased from our useless efforts; and, too cast down for speech, silently gathered up our things and the little effects of those who were lost, preparatory to continuing the descent. When, lo! a mighty arch appeared, rising above the Lyskamm, high into the sky. Pale, colourless, and noiseless, but perfectly sharp and defined, except where it was lost in the clouds, this unearthly apparition seemed like a vision from another world; and almost appalled, we watched with amazement the gradual development of two vast crosses, one on either side. If the Taugwalders had not been the first to perceive it, I should have doubted my senses. They thought it had some connection with the accident, and I, after a while, that it might bear some relation to ourselves. But our movements had no effect upon it. The spectral forms remained motionless. It was a fearful and wonderful sight; unique in my experience, and impressive beyond description, coming at such a moment.

SUNSET

ON MONT BLANC

SIR LESLIE STEPHEN

The Reverend Sir Leslie Stephen (1832–1904) was primarily a literary figure in England; he wrote biographies of Jonathan Swift, Alexander Pope, and Samuel Johnson, contributed to the *Pall Mall Gazette*, published *The History of English Thought in the Eighteenth Century*, and, after joining the Alpine Club in 1858, became editor of the *Alpine Journal* from 1868 to 1872. He was also the father of Virginia Woolf. He was an avid mountain climber, one of the first to establish the English fascination with the rugged natural landscapes of the Swiss Alps. It was perfectly understandable that he would climb Mont Blanc simply because he had heard that the view of the sunset from its peak was unsurpassable. This account of the climb is taken from his book *The Playground of Europe* (1936).

. . .

IT IS TRUE, indeed, that Mont Blanc sometimes is too savage for poetry. He can speak in downright tragic earnestness; and anyone who has been caught in a storm on some of his higher icefields, who has trembled at the deadly swoop of the gale, or at the ominous sound which heralds an avalanche, or at the remorseless settling down of the blinding snow, will agree that at times he passes the limits of the terrible which comes fairly within the range of art. There are times, however, at which one may expect to find precisely the right blending of the sweet and the stern. And in particular, there are those exquisite moments when the sunset is breathing over his calm snowfields its "ardours of rest and love." Watched from beneath, the Alpine glow, as everybody knows, is of exquisite beauty; but unfortunately the spectacle has become a little too popular. The very sunset seems to smell of *Baedeker's Guide*. The flesh is weak and the most sympathetic of human beings is apt to feel a slight sense of revulsion when the French guests at a *table d'hôte* are exclaiming in chorus, *"Magnifique, superbe!"* and the Germans chiming in with *"Wunderschön!"* and the British tourist patting the old mountain on the back, and the American protesting that he has shinier sunsets at home. Not being of a specially sympathetic nature, I had frequently wondered how that glorious spectacle would look from the solitary top of the monarch himself. This summer I was fortunate enough, owing to the judicious arrangements of one of his most famous courtiers—my old friend and comrade M. Gabriel Loppé—to be able to give an answer founded on personal experience. The result was to me so interesting that I shall venture—rash as the attempt may be—to give some account of a phenomenon of extraordinary beauty which has hitherto been witnessed by not more than some half-dozen human beings.

It was in the early morning of August 6, 1873, that I left Chamonix for the purpose. The sun rose on one of those fresh dewy dawns unknown except in the mountains, when the buoyant air seems as it were to penetrate every pore in one's body. I could almost say with Tennyson's Sir Galahad:

> This mortal armour that I wear,
> This weight and size, this heart and eyes,
> Are touch'd and turn'd to finest air.

The heavy, sodden framework of flesh and blood which I languidly dragged along London streets underwent a strange transformation, and it was with scarcely a conscious effort that I breasted the monstrous hill which towered above me. The pine-woods gave out their aromatic scent, and the little glades were deep in ferns, wild-flowers, and strawberries. Even here, the latent terrors of the mountains were kept in mind by the huge boulders which, at some distant day, had crashed like cannonballs through the forest. But the great mountain was not now indulging in one of his ponderous games at bowls, and the soft carpeting of tender vegetation suggested rather luxurious indolence, and, maybe, recalled lazy picnics rather than any more strenuous memories.

Before long, however, we emerged from the forest, and soon the bells of a jolly little company of goats bade us farewell on the limits of the civilised world, as we stepped upon the still frozen glacier and found ourselves fairly in the presence. We were alone with the mighty dome, dazzling our eyes in the brilliant sunshine, and guarded by its sleeping avalanches. Luckily there was no temptation to commit the abomination of walking "against time" or racing any rival caravan of climbers. The whole day was before us, for it would have been undesirable to reach the chilly summit too early; and we could afford the unusual luxury of lounging up Mont Blanc. We took, I hope, full advantage of our opportunities. We could peer into the blue depths of crevasses, so beautiful that one might long for such a grave, were it not for the awkward prospect of having one's bones put under a glass case by the next generation of scientific travellers. We could record in our memories the strange forms of the shattered séracs, those grotesque ice-masses which seem to suggest that the monarch himself has a certain clumsy sense of humour.

We lingered longest on the summit of the Dôme du Goûter, itself a most majestic mountain were it not overawed by its gigantic neighbour. There, on the few ledges which are left exposed in summer, the thunder has left its scars. The lightning's strokes have covered numbers of stones with little glass-like heads, showing that this must be one of its favourite haunts. But on this glorious summer day the lightnings were at rest; and we could peacefully count over the vast wilderness of peaks which already stretched far and wide beneath our feet. The lower mountain ranges appeared to be drawn up in parallel ranks like the sea waves heaved in calm weather by a monotonous ground-swell. Each ridge was blended into a uniform hue by the intervening atmosphere, sharply defined along the summit line, and yet only distinguished from its predecessor and successor by a delicate gradation of tone.

Such a view produces the powerful but shadowy impression which one expects from an opium dream. The vast perspective drags itself out to an horizon so distant as to blend imperceptibly with the lower sky. It has a vague suggestion of rhythmical motion, strangely combined with eternal calm. Drop a pebble into a perfectly still sheet of water; imagine that each ripple is supplanted by a lofty mountain range, of which all detail is lost in purple haze, and that the furthest undulations melt into the mysterious infinite. One gazes with a sense of soothing melancholy as one listens to plaintive modulations of some air of linked "sweetness long drawn out." Far away among the hills we could see long reaches of the peaceful Lake of Geneva, just gleaming through the varying purple; but at our backs the icy crest of the great mountain still rose proudly above us, to remind us that our task was not yet finished. Fortunately for us, scarcely a cloud was to be seen under the enormous concave of the dark blue heavens; a few light streamers of cirrus were moving gently over our heads in those remote abysses from which they never condescend even to the loftiest of Alpine summits. Faint and evanescent as they might be, they possibly had an ominous meaning for the future, but the present was our own; the little puffs of wind that whispered round some lofty ledges were keen enough in quality to remind us of possible frost-bites, but they had scarcely force enough to extinguish a lucifer match.

Carefully calculating our time, we advanced along the "dromedary's hump" and stepped upon the culminating ridge of the mountain about an hour before sunset. We had time to collect ourselves, to awake our powers of observation, and to prepare for the grand spectacle, for which preparations were already being made. There had been rehearsals enough in all conscience to secure a perfect performance. For millions of ages the lamps had been lighted and the transparencies had been shown with no human eye to observe or hand to applaud. Twice, I believe only twice, before, an audience had taken its place in this lofty gallery; but on one of those occasions, at least, the observers had been too unwell to do justice to the spectacle. The other party, of which the chief member was a French man of science, Dr. Martens, had been obliged to retreat hastily before the lights were extinguished; but their fragmentary account had excited our curiosity, and we had the pleasure of verifying the most striking phenomenon which they described.

And now we waited eagerly for the performance to commence; the cold was sufficient to freeze the wine in our bottles, but in still air the cold is but little felt, and by walking briskly up and down and adopting the gymnastic exercise in which the London cabman delights in cold weather, we were able to keep up a sufficient degree of circulation. I say "we," but I am libelling the most enthusiastic member of the party. Loppé sat resolutely on the snow, at the risk, as we might have thought, of following the example of Lot's wife. Superior, as it appeared, to all the frailties which beset the human frame suddenly plunged into a temperature I know not how many degrees below freezing-point, he worked with ever increasing fury in a desperate attempt to fix upon canvas some of the magic beauties of the scene. Glancing from earth to heaven and from north to south, sketching with breathless rapidity the appearance of the eastern ranges, then wheeling round like a weathercock to make hasty notes of the western clouds, breaking out at times into uncontrollable exclamations of delight, or reproving his thoughtless companions when their opaque bodies eclipsed a whole quarter of the heavens, he enjoyed, I should fancy, an hour of as keen delight as not often occurs to an enthusiastic lover of the sublime in nature. We laughed, envied, and admired, and he escaped frost-bites.

I wish that I could substitute his canvas—though, to say the truth, I fear it would exhibit a slight confusion of the points of the compass—for my words; but, as that is impossible, I must endeavour briefly to indicate the most impressive features of the scenery. My readers must kindly set their imaginations to work in aid of feeble language; for even the most eloquent language is but a poor substitute for a painter's brush, and a painter's brush lags far behind these grandest aspects of nature. The easiest way of obtaining the impression is to follow in my steps; for, in watching a sunset from Mont Blanc one feels that one is passing one of those rare moments of life at which all the surrounding scenery is instantaneously and indelibly photographed on the mental retina by a process which no second-hand operation can even dimly transfer to others. To explain its nature requires a word or two of preface.

The ordinary view from Mont Blanc is not specially picturesque—and for sufficient reason. The architect has concentrated his whole energies in producing a single impression. Everything has been so arranged as to intensify the sense of vast height and an illimitable horizon. In a good old guide-book I have read, on the authority (I think) of Pliny, that the highest mountain in the world is 300,000 feet above the sea; and one is apt to fancy, on ascending Mont Blanc, that the guess is not so far out. The effect is perfectly unique in the Alps; but it is produced at a certain sacrifice. All dangerous rivals have been removed to such a distance as to become apparently insignificant. No grand mass can be admitted into the foreground; for the sense of vast size is gradually forced upon you by the infinite multiplicity of detail.

Mont Blanc must be like an Asiatic despot, alone and supreme, with all inferior peaks reverently crouched at his feet. If a man, previously as ignorant of geography as a boy who has just left a public school, could be transported for a moment to the summit, his impression would be that the Alps resembled a village of a hundred hovels grouped around a stupendous cathedral. Fully to appreciate this effect requires a certain familiarity with Alpine scenery, for otherwise the effect produced is a dwarfing of the inferior mountains into pettiness instead of an exaltation of Mont Blanc into almost portentous magnificence. Grouped around you at unequal distances lie innumerable white patches, looking like the tented encampments of scattered army corps. Hold up a glove at arm's length, and it will cover the whole of such a group. On the boundless plain beneath (I say "plain," for the greatest mountain system of Europe appears to have subsided into a rather uneven plain), it is a mere spot, a trifling dent upon the huge shield on whose central boss you are placed. But you know, though at first you can hardly realise the knowledge, that that insignificant discoloration represents a whole mountain district. One spot, for example, represents the clustered peaks of the Bernese Oberland; a block, as big as a pebble, is the soaring Jungfrau, the terrible mother of avalanches; a barely distinguishable wrinkle is the reverse of those snowy wastes of the Blümlisalp, which seem to be suspended above the terrace of Berne, thirty miles away; and that little whitish stream represents the greatest ice-stream of the Alps, the huge Aletsch Glacier, whose monstrous proportions have been impressed upon you by hours of laborious plodding. One patch contains the main sources from which the Rhine descends to the German ocean, two or three more overlook the Italian plains and encircle the basin of the Po; from a more distant group flows the Danube, and from your feet the snows melt to supply the Rhône. You feel that you are in some sense looking down upon Europe from Rotterdam to Venice and from Varna to Marseilles. The vividness of the impression depends entirely upon the degree to which you can realise the immense size of all these immeasurable details.

Now, in the morning, the usual time for an ascent, the details are necessarily vague, because the noblest part of the view lies between the sun and the spectator. But in the evening light each ridge, and peak, and glacier stands out with startling distinctness, and each, therefore, is laden with its weight of old association. There, for example, was the grim Matterhorn: its angular dimensions were of infinitesimal minuteness; it would puzzle a mathematician to say how small a space its image would occupy on his retina; but, within that small space, its form was defined with exquisite accuracy; and we could recognise the precise configuration of the wild labyrinth of rocky ridges up which the earlier adventurers forced their way from the Italian side. And thus we not only knew, but felt that at our feet was lying a vast slice of the map of Europe. The effect was to exaggerate the apparent height, till the view had about it something portentous and unnatural: it seemed to be such a view as could be granted not even to mountaineers of earthly mould, but rather to some genie from the *Arabian Nights*, flying high above a world tinted with the magical colouring of old romance.

Thus distinctly drawn, though upon so minute a scale, every rock and slope preserved its true value, and the impression of stupendous height became almost oppressive as it was forced upon the imagination that a whole world of mountains, each of them a mighty mass in itself, lay couched far beneath our feet, reaching across the whole diameter of the vast panorama. And now, whilst occupied in drinking in that strange sensation, and allowing our minds to recover their equilibrium from the first staggering shock of astonishment, began the strange spectacle of which we were the sole witnesses. One long delicate cloud, suspended in mid-air just below the sun, was gradually adorning itself with prismatic colouring. Round the limitless horizon ran a faint fog-bank, unfortunately not quite thick enough to produce that depth of colouring which sometimes makes an Alpine sunset inexpressibly gorgeous.

The weather—it was the only complaint we had to make—erred on the side of fineness. But the colouring was brilliant enough to prevent any thoughts of serious disappointment. The long series of western ranges melted into a uniform hue as the sun declined in their rear. Amidst their folds the Lake of Geneva became suddenly lighted up in a faint yellow gleam. To the east a blue gauze seemed to cover valley by valley as they sank into night and the intervening ridges rose with increasing distinctness, or rather it seemed that some fluid of exquisite delicacy of colour and substance was flooding all the lower country beneath the great mountains. Peak by peak the high snowfields caught the rosy glow and shone like signal-fires across the dim breadths of delicate twilight. Like Xerxes, we looked over the countless host sinking into rest, but with the rather different reflection, that a hundred years hence they would probably be doing much the same thing, whilst we should have long ceased to take any interest in the performance.

And suddenly began a more startling phenomenon. A vast cone, with its apex pointing away from us, seemed to be suddenly cut out from the world beneath; night was within its borders and the twilight still all round; the blue mists were quenched where it fell, and for the instant we could scarcely tell what was the origin of this strange appearance. Some unexpected change seemed to have taken place in the programme; as though a great fold in the curtain had suddenly given way, and dropped on to part of the scenery. Of course a moment's reflection explained the meaning of this uncanny intruder; it was the giant shadow of Mont Blanc, testifying to his supremacy over all meaner eminences. It is difficult to say how sharply marked was the outline, and how startling was the contrast between this pyramid of darkness and the faintly-lighted spaces beyond its influence; a huge inky blot seemed to have suddenly fallen upon the landscape. As we gazed we could see it move. It swallowed up ridge by ridge, and its sharp point crept steadily from one landmark to another down the broad Valley of Aosta. We were standing, in fact, on the point of the gnomon of a gigantic sundial, the face of which was formed by thousands of square miles of mountain and valley. So clear was the outline that, if figures had been scrawled upon glaciers and ridges, we could have told the time to a second; indeed, we were half-inclined to look for our own shadows at a distance so great that the whole villages would be represented by a scarcely distinguishable speck of colouring.

The huge shadow, looking ever more strange and magical, struck the distant Becca di Nona, and then climbed into the dark region where the broader shadow of the world was rising into the eastern sky. By some singular effect of perspective, rays of darkness seemed to be converging from above our heads to a point immediately above the apex of the shadowy cone. For a time it seemed that there was a kind of anti-sun in the east, pouring out not light, but deep shadow as it rose. The apex soon reached the horizon, and then to our surprise began climbing the distant sky. Would it never stop, and was Mont Blanc capable of overshadowing not only the earth but the sky? For a minute or two I fancied, in a bewildered way, that this unearthly object would fairly rise from the ground and climb upwards to the zenith. But rapidly the lights went out upon the great army of mountains; the snow all round took the livid hue which immediately succeeds an Alpine sunset, and almost at a blow the shadow of Mont Blanc was swallowed up in the general shade of night.

MOUNT SHASTA

JOHN MUIR

Born in Wisconsin in 1838, Muir set out on his "thousand-mile walk" from Indiana to the Gulf of Mexico in 1865 and ended up in California, where he ran a fruit farm in the Alhambra Valley and campaigned for the preservation of California's wilderness. He was largely responsible for the establishment of Yosemite National Park in 1890 and was popularly known as "John of the Mountains." The following story is from his 1888 book *Picturesque California*; Muir didn't so much climb mountains as amble up them, stopping to observe wildlife, admire the view, and lie down to sleep if the mood struck him, as it did during snowstorms on Mount Shasta in November of 1874 and again in April of 1875.

. . .

TOWARD THE END of summer, after a light, open winter, one may reach the summit of Mount Shasta without passing over much snow, by keeping on the crest of a long narrow ridge, mostly bare, that extends from near the camp-ground at the timber-line. But on my first excursion to the summit the whole mountain, down to its low swelling base, was smoothly laden with loose fresh snow, presenting a most glorious mass of winter mountain scenery, in the midst of which I scrambled and revelled or lay snugly snowbound, enjoying the fertile clouds and the snow-bloom in all their growing, drifting grandeur.

I had walked from Redding, sauntering leisurely from station to station along the old Oregon stage road, the better to see the rocks and plants, birds and people, by the way, tracing the rushing Sacramento to its fountains around icy Shasta. The first rains had fallen on the lowlands, and the first snows on the mountains, and everything was fresh and bracing, while an abundance of balmy sunshine filled all the noonday hours. It was the calm afterglow that usually succeeds the first storm of the winter. I met many of the birds that had reared their young and spent their summer in the Shasta woods and chaparral. They were then on their way south to their winter homes, leading their young full-fledged and about as large and strong as the parents. Squirrels, dry and elastic after the storms, were busy about their stores of pine nuts, and the latest goldenrods were still in bloom, though it was now past the middle of October. The grand color glow—the autumnal jubilee of ripe leaves— was past prime, but, freshened by the rain, was still making a fine show along the banks of the river and in the ravines and the dells of the smaller streams.

At the salmon-hatching establishment on the McCloud River I halted a week to examine the limestone belt, grandly developed there, to learn what I could of the inhabitants of the river and its banks, and to give time for the fresh snow that I knew had fallen on the mountain to settle somewhat, with a view to making the ascent. A pedestrian on these mountain roads, especially so late in the year, is sure to excite curiosity, and many were the interrogations concerning my ramble. When I said that I was simply taking a walk, and that icy Shasta was my mark, I was invariably admonished that I had come on a dangerous quest. The time was far too late, the snow was too loose and deep to climb, and I should be lost in drifts and slides. When I hinted that new snow was beautiful and storms not so bad as they were called, my advisers shook their heads in token of superior knowledge and declared the ascent of "Shasta Butte" through loose snow impossible...

When I arrived at Sisson's everything was quiet. The last of the summer visitors had flitted long before, and the deer and bears also were beginning to seek their winter homes. My barometer and the sighing winds and filmy, half-transparent clouds that dimmed the sunshine gave notice of the approach of another storm, and I was in haste to be off and get myself established somewhere in the midst of it, whether the summit was to be attained or not. Sisson, who is a mountaineer, speedily fitted me out for storm or calm as only a mountaineer could, with warm blankets and a week's provisions so generous in quantity and kind that they easily might have been made to last a month in case of my being closely snowbound. Well I knew the weariness of snow-climbing, and the frosts, and the dangers of mountaineering so late in the year; therefore I could not ask a guide to go with me, even had one been willing. All I wanted was to have blankets and provisions deposited as far up in the timber as the snow would permit a pack-animal to go. There I could build a storm nest and lie warm, and make raids up and around the mountain in accordance with the weather.

Setting out on the afternoon of November first, with Jerome Fay, mountaineer and guide, in charge of the animals, I was soon plodding wearily upward through the muffled winter woods, the snow of course growing steadily deeper and looser, so that we had to break a trail. The animals began to get discouraged, and after night and darkness came on they became entangled in a bed of rough lava, where, breaking through four or five feet of mealy snow, their feet were caught between angular boulders. Here they were in danger of being lost, but after we had removed packs and saddles and assisted their efforts with ropes, they all escaped to the side of a ridge about 1,000 feet below the timber-line.

To go farther was out of the question, so we were compelled to camp as best we could. A pitch-pine fire speedily changed the temperature and shed a blaze of light on the wild lava-slope and the straggling storm-bent pines around us. Melted snow answered for coffee, and we had plenty of venison to roast. Toward midnight I rolled myself in my blankets, slept an hour and a half, arose and ate more venison, tied two days' provisions to my belt, and set out for the summit, hoping to reach it ere the coming storm should fall. Jerome accompanied me a little distance above camp and indicated the way as well as he could in the darkness. He seemed loath to leave me, but, being reassured that I was at home and required no care, he bade me goodbye and returned to camp, ready to lead his animals down the mountain at daybreak.

After I was above the dwarf pines, it was fine practice pushing up the broad unbroken slopes of snow, alone in the solemn silence of the night. Half the sky was clouded; in the other half the stars sparkled icily in the keen, frosty air; while everywhere the glorious wealth of snow fell away from the summit of the cone in flowing folds, more extensive and continuous than any I had ever seen before. When day dawned the clouds were crawling slowly and becoming more massive, but gave no intimation of immediate danger, and I pushed on faithfully, though holding myself well in hand, ready to return to the timber; for it was easy to see that the storm was not far off. The mountain rises 10,000 feet above the general level of the country, in blank exposure to the deep upper currents of the sky, and no labyrinth of peaks and canyons I had ever been in seemed to me so dangerous as these immense slopes, bare against the sky.

The frost was intense, and drifting snow-dust made breathing at times rather difficult. The snow was as dry as meal, and the finer particles drifted freely, rising high in the air, while the larger portions of the crystals rolled like sand. I frequently sank to my armpits between buried blocks of loose lava, but generally only to my knees. When tired with walking I still wallowed slowly upward on all fours. The steepness of the slope—thirty-five degrees in some places—made any kind of progress fatiguing, while small avalanches were being constantly set in motion in the steepest places. But the bracing air and the sublime beauty of the snowy expanse thrilled every nerve and made absolute exhaustion impossible. I seemed to be walking and wallowing in a cloud; but, holding steadily onward, by half-past ten o'clock I had gained the highest summit.

I held my commanding foothold in the sky for two hours, gazing on the glorious landscapes spread map-like around the immense horizon, and tracing the outlines of the ancient lava-streams extending far into the surrounding plains, and the pathways of vanished glaciers of which Shasta had been the center. But, as I had left my coat in camp for the sake of having my limbs free in climbing, I soon was cold. The wind increased in violence, raising the snow in magnificent drifts that were drawn out in the form of wavering banners blowing in the sun. Toward the end of my stay a succession of small clouds struck against the summit rocks like drifting icebergs, darkening the air as they passed, and producing a chill as definite and sudden as if ice-water had been dashed in my face. This is the kind of cloud in which snow-flowers grow, and I turned and fled.

Finding that I was not closely pursued, I ventured to take time on the way down for a visit to the head of the Whitney Glacier and the "Crater Butte." After I had reached the end of the main summit ridge the descent was but little more than one continuous soft, mealy, muffled slide, most luxurious and rapid, though the hissing, swishing speed attained was obscured in great part by flying snow-dust—a marked contrast to the boring seal-wallowing upward struggle. I reached camp about an hour before dusk, hollowed a strip of loose ground in the lee of a large block of red lava, where firewood was abundant, rolled myself in my blankets, and went to sleep.

Next morning, having slept little the night before the ascent and being weary with climbing after the excitement was over, I slept late. Then, awaking suddenly, my eyes opened on one of the most beautiful and sublime scenes I ever enjoyed. A boundless wilderness of storm-clouds of different degrees of ripeness were congregated over all the lower landscape for thousands of square miles, colored grey, and purple, and pearl, and deep-glowing white, amid which I seemed to be floating; while the great white cone of the mountain above was all aglow in the free, blazing sunshine. It seemed not so much an ocean as a *land* of clouds—undulating hill and dale, smooth purple plains, and silvery mountains of cumuli, range over range, diversified with peak and dome and hollow fully brought out in light and shade.

I gazed enchanted, but cold gray masses, drifting like dust on a wind-swept plain, began to shut out the light, forerunners of the coming storm I had been so anxiously watching. I made haste to gather as much wood as possible, snugging it as a shelter around my bed. The storm side of my blankets was fastened down with stakes to reduce as much as possible the sifting-in of drift and the danger of being blown away. The precious bread-sack was placed safely as a pillow, and when at length the first flakes fell I was exultingly ready to welcome them. Most of my firewood was more than half rosin and would blaze in the face of the fiercest drifting; the winds could not demolish my bed, and my bread could be made to last indefinitely; while in case of need I had the means of making snowshoes and could retreat or hold my ground as I pleased.

Presently the storm broke forth into full snowy bloom, and the thronging crystals darkened the air. The wind swept past in hissing floods, grinding the snow into meal and sweeping down into the hollows in enormous drifts all the heavier particles, while the finer dust was sifted through the sky, increasing the icy gloom. But my fire glowed bravely as if in glad defiance of the drift to quench it, and, notwithstanding but little trace of my nest could be seen after the snow had levelled and buried it, I was snug and warm, and the passionate uproar produced a glad excitement.

Day after day the storm continued, piling snow on snow in weariless abundance. There were short periods of quiet, when the sun would seem to look eagerly down through rents in the clouds, as if to know how the work was advancing. During these calm intervals I replenished my fire—sometimes without leaving the nest, for fire and woodpile were so near this could easily be done—or busied myself with my notebook, watching the gestures of the trees in taking the snow, examining separate crystals under a lens, and learning the methods of their deposition as an enduring fountain for the streams. Several times, when the storm ceased for a few minutes, a Douglas squirrel came frisking from the foot of a clump of dwarf pines, moving in sudden interrupted spurts over the bossy snow; then, without any apparent guidance, he would dig rapidly into the drift where were buried some grains of barley that the horses had left. The Douglas squirrel does not strictly belong to these upper woods, and I was surprised to see him out in such weather. The mountain sheep also, quite a large flock of them, came to my camp and took shelter beside a clump of matted dwarf pines a little above my nest.

The storm lasted about a week, but before it was ended Sisson became alarmed and sent up the guide with animals to see what had become of me and recover the camp outfit. The news spread that "there was a man on the mountain," and he must surely have perished, and Sisson was blamed for allowing any one to attempt climbing in such weather; while I was as safe as anybody in the lowlands, lying like a squirrel in a warm, fluffy nest, busied about my own affairs and wishing only to be let alone.

THE NEXT SPRING, on the other side of this eventful winter, I saw and felt still more of the Shasta snow. For then it was my fortune to get into the very heart of a Shasta storm and to be held in it for a long time.

On the 28th of April [1875] I led a party up the mountain for the purpose of making a survey of the summit with reference to the location of the Geodetic monument. On the 30th, accompanied by Jerome Fay, I made another ascent to make some barometrical observations, the day intervening between the two ascents being devoted to establishing a camp on the extreme edge of the timber line. Here, on our red trachyte bed, we obtained two hours of shallow sleep broken for occasional glimpses of the keen, starry night. At two o'clock we rose, breakfasted on a warmed tin-cupful of coffee and a piece of frozen venison broiled on the coals, and started for the summit. Up to this time there was nothing in sight that betokened the approach of a storm; but on gaining the summit, we saw toward Lassen's Butte hundreds of square miles of white cumuli boiling dreamily in the sunshine far beneath us, and causing no alarm.

The slight weariness of the ascent was soon rested away, and our glorious morning in the sky promised nothing but enjoyment. At 9 AM the dry thermometer stood at 34° in the shade and rose steadily until at 1 PM it stood at 50°, probably influenced somewhat by radiation from the sun-warmed cliffs. A common bumblebee, not at all benumbed, zigzagged vigorously about our heads for a few moments, as if unconscious of the fact that the nearest honey flower was a mile beneath him.

In the meantime clouds were growing down in Shasta Valley—massive swelling cumuli, displaying delicious tones of purple and grey in the hollows of their sun-beaten bosses. Extending gradually southward around on both sides of Shasta, these at length united with the older field towards Lassen's Butte, thus encircling Mount Shasta in one continuous cloud-zone. Rhett and Klamath Lakes were eclipsed beneath clouds scarcely less brilliant than their own silvery disks. The Modoc Lava Beds, many a snow-laden peak far north in Oregon, the Scott and Trinity and Siskiyou Mountains, the peaks of the

Sierra, the blue Coast Range, Shasta Valley, the dark forests filling the valley of the Sacramento, all in turn were obscured or
buried, leaving the lofty cone on which we stood solitary in the
sunshine between two skies—a sky of spotless blue above, a sky
of glittering cloud beneath. The creative sun shone glorious on
the vast expanse of cloudland; hill and dale, mountain and valley springing into existence responsive to his rays and steadily
developing in beauty and individuality. One huge mountain-
cone of cloud, corresponding to Mount Shasta in these newborn
cloud-ranges, rose close alongside with a visible motion, its firm,
polished bosses seeming so near and substantial that we almost
fancied that we might leap down upon them from where we
stood and make our way to the lowlands. No hint was given, by
anything in their appearance, of the fleeting character of these
most sublime and beautiful cloud mountains. On the contrary
they impressed one as being lasting additions to the landscape.

The weather of the springtime and summer, throughout
the Sierra in general, is usually varied by slight local rains and
dustings of snow, most of which are obviously far too joyous
and life-giving to be regarded as storms—single clouds growing in the sunny sky, ripening in an hour, showering the heated
landscape, and passing away like a thought, leaving no visible
bodily remains to stain the sky. Snowstorms of the same gentle kind abound among the high peaks, but in spring they not
unfrequently attain larger proportions, assuming a violence and
energy of expression scarcely surpassed by those bred in the
depths of winter. Such was the storm now gathering about us.

It began to declare itself shortly after noon, suggesting to us the idea of at once seeking our safe camp in the timber and abandoning the purpose of making an observation of the barometer at 3 PM—two having already been made, at 9 AM, and 12 noon, while simultaneous observations were made at Strawberry Valley. Jerome peered at short intervals over the ridge, contemplating the rising clouds with anxious gestures in the rough wind, and at length declared that if we did not make a speedy escape we should be compelled to pass the rest of the day and night on the summit. But anxiety to complete my observations stifled my own instinctive promptings to retreat, and held me to my work. No inexperienced person was depending on me, and I told Jerome that we two mountaineers should be able to make our way down through any storm likely to fall.

Presently thin, fibrous films of cloud began to blow directly over the summit from north to south, drawn out in long fairy webs like carded wool, forming and dissolving as if by magic. The wind twisted them into ringlets and whirled them in a succession of graceful convolutions like the outside sprays of Yosemite Falls in flood-time; then, sailing out into the thin azure over the precipitous brink of the ridge they were drifted together like wreaths of foam on a river. These higher and finer cloud fabrics were evidently produced by the chilling of the air from its own expansion caused by the upward deflection of the wind against the slopes of the mountain. They steadily increased on the north rim of the cone, forming at length a thick, opaque, ill-defined embankment from the icy meshes of which snow-flowers began to fall, alternating with hail. The sky speedily darkened, and just as I had completed my last observation and boxed my instruments ready for the descent, the storm began in serious earnest. At first the cliffs were beaten with hail, every stone of which, as far as I could see, was regular in form, six-sided pyramids with rounded base, rich and sumptuous looking, and fashioned with loving care, yet seemingly thrown away on those desolate crags down which they went rolling, falling, sliding in a network of curious streams.

After we had forced our way down the ridge and past the group of hissing fumaroles, the storm became inconceivably violent. The thermometer fell 22° in a few minutes, and soon dropped below zero. The hail gave place to snow, and darkness came on like night. The wind, rising to the highest pitch of violence, boomed and surged amid the desolate crags; lightning-flashes in quick succession cut the gloomy darkness; and the thunders, the most tremendously loud and appalling I ever heard, made an almost continuous roar, stroke following stroke in quick, passionate succession, as though the mountain were being rent to its foundations and the fires of the old volcano were breaking forth again.

Could we at once have begun to descend the snow-slopes leading to the timber, we might have made good our escape, however dark and wild the storm. As it was, we had first to make our way along a dangerous ridge nearly a mile and a half long, flanked in many places by steep ice-slopes at the head of the Whitney Glacier on one side and by shattered precipices on the other. Apprehensive of this coming darkness, I had taken the precaution, when the storm began, to make the most dangerous points clear to my mind, and to mark their relations with reference to the direction of the wind. When, therefore, the darkness came on, and the bewildering drift, I felt confident that we could force our way through it with no other guidance. After passing the "Hot Springs" I halted in the lee of a lava-block to let Jerome, who had fallen a little behind, come up. Here he opened a council in which, under circumstances sufficiently exciting but without evincing any bewilderment, he maintained, in opposition to my views, that it was impossible to proceed. He firmly refused to make the venture to find the camp, while I, aware of the dangers that would necessarily attend our efforts, and conscious of being the cause of his present peril, decided not to leave him.

Our discussions ended, Jerome made a dash from the shelter of the lava-block and began forcing his way back against the wind to the "Hot Springs," wavering and struggling to resist being carried away, as if he were fording a rapid stream. After waiting and watching in vain for some flaw in the storm that might be urged as a new argument in favor of attempting the descent, I was compelled to follow. 'Here," said Jerome, as we shivered in the midst of the hissing, sputtering fumaroles, "we shall be safe from frost."

"Yes," said I, "we can lie in this mud and steam and sludge, warm at least on one side; but how can we protect our lungs from the acid gases, and how, after our clothing is saturated, shall we be able to reach camp without freezing, even after the storm is over? We shall have to wait for sunshine, and when will it come?"

The tempered area to which we had committed ourselves extended over about one fourth of an acre; but it was only about an eighth of an inch in thickness, for the scalding gas-jets were shorn off close to the ground by the oversweeping flood of frosty wind. And how lavishly the snow fell only mountaineers may know. The crisp crystal flowers seemed to touch one another and fairly to thicken the tremendous blast that carried them. This was the bloom-time, the summer of the cloud, and never before have I seen even a mountain cloud flowering so profusely.

When the bloom of the Shasta chaparral is falling, the ground is sometimes covered for hundreds of square miles to a depth of half an inch. But the bloom of this fertile snow-cloud grew and matured and fell to a depth of two feet in a few hours. Some crystals landed with their rays almost perfect, but most of them were worn and broken by striking against one another, or by rolling on the ground. The touch of these snow-flowers in calm weather is infinitely gentle—glinting, swaying, set-tling silently in the dry mountain air, or massed in flakes soft and downy. To lie out alone in the mountains of a still night and be touched by the first of these small silent messengers from the sky is a memorable experience, and the fineness of that touch none will forget. But the storm-blast laden with crisp, sharp snow seems to crush and bruise and stupefy with its multitude of stings, and compels the bravest to turn and flee.

The snow fell without abatement until an hour or two after what seemed to be the natural darkness of the night. Up to the time the storm first broke on the summit its development was remarkably gentle. There was a deliberate growth of clouds, a weaving of translucent tissue above, then the roar of the wind and the thunder, and the darkening flight of snow. Its subsidence was not less sudden. The clouds broke and vanished, not a crystal was left in the sky, and the stars shone out with pure and tranquil radiance.

During the storm we lay on our backs so as to present as little surface as possible to the wind, and to let the drift pass over us. The mealy snow sifted into the folds of our clothing and in many places reached the skin. We were glad at first to see the snow packing about us, hoping it would deaden the force of the wind, but it soon froze into a stiff, crusty heap as the temperature fell, rather augmenting our novel misery.

When the heat became unendurable, on some spot where steam was escaping through the sludge, we tried to stop it with snow and mud, or shifted a little at a time by shoving with our heels; for to stand in blank exposure to the fearful wind in our frozen-and-broiled condition seemed certain death. The acrid incrustations sublimed from the escaping gases frequently gave way, opening new vents to scald us; and, fearing that if at any time the wind should fall, carbonic acid, which often formed a considerable portion of the gaseous exhalations of volcanoes, might collect in sufficient quantities to cause sleep and death, I warned Jerome against forgetting himself for a single moment, even should his sufferings admit of such a thing.

Accordingly, when during the long, dreary watches of the night we roused from a state of half-consciousness, we called each other by name in a frightened, startled way, each fearing the other might be benumbed or dead. The ordinary sensations of cold give but a faint conception of that which comes on after hard climbing with want of food and sleep in such exposure as this. Life is then seen to be a fire, that now smoulders, now brightens, and may be easily quenched. The weary hours wore away like dim half-forgotten years, so long and eventful they seemed, though we did nothing but suffer. Still the pain was not always of that bitter, intense kind that precludes thought and takes away all capacity for enjoyment. A sort of dreamy stupor came on at times in which we fancied we saw dry, resinous logs suitable for campfires, just as after going days without food men fancy they see bread.

Frozen, blistered, famished, benumbed, our bodies seemed lost to us at times—all dead but the eyes. For the duller and fainter we became the clearer was our vision, though only in momentary glimpses. Then, after the sky cleared, we gazed at the stars, blessed immortals of light, shining with marvellous brightness with long lance rays, near-looking and new-looking, as if never seen before. Again they would look familiar and remind us of star-gazing at home. Oftentimes imagination coming into play would present charming pictures of the warm zone below, mingled with others near and far. Then the bitter wind and the drift would break the blissful vision and dreary pains cover us like clouds. "Are you suffering much?" Jerome would inquire with pitiful faintness.

"Yes," I would say, striving to keep my voice brave, "frozen and burned; but never mind, Jerome, the night will wear away at last, and tomorrow we go a-Maying, and what campfires we will make, and what sun-baths we will take!"

The frost grew more and more intense, and we became icy and covered over with a crust of frozen snow, as if we had lain cast away in the drift all winter. In about thirteen hours—every hour like a year—day began to dawn, but it was long ere the summit's rocks were touched by the sun. No clouds were visible from where we lay, yet the morning was dull and blue, and bitterly frosty; and hour after hour passed by while we eagerly watched the pale light stealing down the ridge to the hollow where we lay. But there was not a trace of that warm, flushing sunrise splendor we so long had hoped for.

As the time drew near to make an effort to reach camp, we became concerned to know what strength was left us, and whether or no we could walk; for we had lain flat all this time without once rising to our feet. Mountaineers, however, always find in themselves a reserve of power after great exhaustion. It is a kind of second life, available only in emergencies like this; and, having proved its existence, I had no great fear that either of us would fail, though one of my arms was already benumbed and hung powerless.

At length, after the temperature was somewhat mitigated on this memorable first of May, we arose and began to struggle homeward. Our frozen trousers could scarcely be made to bend at the knee, and we waded the snow with difficulty. The summit ridge was fortunately wind-swept and nearly bare, so we were not compelled to lift our feet high, and on reaching the long home slopes laden with loose snow we made rapid progress, sliding and shuffling and pitching headlong, our feebleness accelerating rather than diminishing our speed. When we had descended some 3,000 feet the sunshine warmed our backs and we began to revive. At 10 AM we reached the timber and were safe.

Half an hour later we heard Sisson shouting down among the firs, coming with horses to take us to the hotel. After breaking a trail through the snow as far as possible he had tied his animals and walked up. We had been so long without food that we cared but little about eating, but we eagerly drank the coffee he prepared for us. Our feet were frozen, and thawing them was painful, and had to be done very slowly by keeping them buried in soft snow for several hours, which avoided permanent damage. Five thousand feet below the summit we found only three inches of new snow, and at the base of the mountain only a slight shower of rain had fallen, showing how local our storm had been, notwithstanding its terrific fury. Our feet were wrapped in sacking, and we were soon mounted and on our way down into the thick sunshine—"God's Country," as Sisson calls the Chaparral Zone. In two hours' ride the last snow-bank was left behind. Violets appeared along the edges of the trail, and the chaparral was coming into bloom, with young lilies and larkspurs about the open places in rich profusion. How beautiful seemed the golden sunbeams streaming through the woods between the warm brown boles of the cedars and pines! All my friends among the birds and plants seemed like *old* friends, and we felt like speaking to every one of them as we passed, as if we had been a long time away in some far, strange country.

In the afternoon we reached Strawberry Valley and fell asleep. Next morning we seemed to have risen from the dead. My bedroom was flooded with sunshine, and from the window I saw the great white Shasta cone clad in forests and clouds and bearing them loftily in the sky. Everything seemed full and radiant with the freshness and beauty and enthusiasm of youth. Sisson's children came in with flowers and covered my bed, and the storm on the mountain-top vanished like a dream.

THE HOLINESS
OF MOUNTAINS

CARL JUNG

Carl Jung's life (1875–1961) spanned enormous changes in civilization's attitude toward Nature, beginning at a time when Darwinism was offering new interpretations of humankind's role in the natural order and including a period when wilderness was threatened by exploitation and degradation. Jung believed that humanity took "a wrong turn" when it lost contact with its past and with "the collective unconscious," which, he said, "is simply Nature." The following account, from *Memories, Dreams, Reflections*, is of Jung's visit to Taos, New Mexico, in 1925, to study native cultures that had maintained their connection with ancestral knowledge.

. . .

I STOOD BY the river and looked up at the mountains, which rise almost another six thousand feet above the plateau. I was just thinking that this was the roof of the American continent, and that people lived here in the face of the sun like the Indians who stood wrapped in blankets on the highest roofs of the

57

pueblo, mute and absorbed in the sight of the sun. Suddenly a deep voice, vibrant with suppressed emotion, spoke from behind me into my left ear: "Do you not think that all life comes from the mountain?" An elderly Indian had come up to me, inaudible in his moccasins, and had asked me this heaven knows how far-reaching question: A glance at the river pouring down from the mountain showed me the outward image that had engendered this conclusion. Obviously all life came from the mountain, for where there is water, there is life. Nothing could be more obvious. In his question I felt a swelling emotion connected with the word "mountain," and thought of the tale of secret rites celebrated on the mountain. I replied, "Everyone can see that you speak the truth.". . .

I observed that the Pueblo Indians, reluctant as they were to speak about anything concerning their religion, talked with great readiness and intensity about their relations with the Americans. "Why," Mountain Lake said, "do the Americans not leave us alone? Why do they want to forbid our dances? Why do they make difficulties when we want to take our young people from school in order to lead them to the *kiva* (site of the rituals), and instruct them in our religion? We do nothing to harm the Americans!" After a prolonged silence he continued, "The Americans want to stamp out our religion. Why can they not let us alone? What we do, we do not only for ourselves but for the Americans also. Yes, we do it for the whole world. Everyone benefits by it."

I could observe from his excitement that he was alluding to some extremely important element of his religion. I therefore asked him: "You think, then, that what you do in your religion benefits the whole world?" He replied with great animation, "Of course. If we did not do it, what would become of the world?" And with a significant gesture he pointed at the sun...

I then realized on what the "dignity," the tranquil composure of the individual Indian, was founded. It springs from his being a son of the sun; his life is cosmologically meaningful, for he helps the father and preserver of all life in his daily rise and descent. If we set against this our own self-justifications, the meaning of our own lives as it is formulated by our reason, we cannot help but see our poverty. Out of sheer envy we are obliged to smile at the Indians' naïveté and to plume ourselves on our cleverness; for otherwise we would discover how impoverished and down at the heels we are. Knowledge does not enrich us; it removes us more and more from the mythic world in which we were once at home by right of birth.

If for a moment we put away all European rationalism and transport ourselves into the clear mountain air of that solitary plateau, which drops off on one side into the broad continental prairies and on the other into the Pacific Ocean; if we also set aside our intimate knowledge of the world and exchange it for a horizon that seems immeasurable, and an ignorance of what lies beyond it, we will begin to achieve an inner comprehension of the Pueblo Indian's point of view. "All life comes from the mountain" is immediately convincing to him, and he is equally certain that he lives upon the roof of an immeasurable world, closest to God. He above all others has the Divinity's ear, and his ritual act will reach the distant sun soonest of all. The holiness of mountains, the revelation of Yahweh upon Sinai, the inspiration that Nietzche was vouchsafed in the Engadine—all speak the same language. The idea, absurd to us, that a ritual act can magically affect the sun is, upon closer examination, no less irrational but far more familiar to us than might at first be assumed. Our Christian religion—like every other, incidentally—is permeated by the idea that special acts or a special kind of action can influence God—for example, through certain rites or by prayer, or by a morality pleasing to the Divinity.

The ritual acts of man are an answer and reaction to the action of God upon man; and perhaps they are not only that, but are also intended to be "activating," a form of magic coercion. That man feels capable of formulating valid replies to the overpowering influence of God, and that he can render back something which is essential even to God, induces pride, for it raises the human individual to the dignity of a metaphysical factor. "God and us"—even if it is only an unconscious *sous-entendu*—this equation no doubt underlies that enviable serenity of the Pueblo Indian. Such a man is in the fullest sense of the word in his proper place.

THE MOUNTAINS
OF THE MOON

JOHN BUCHAN

Novelist, biographer, statesman, and sportsman, John Buchan (First Baron Tweedsmuir) exemplified the Renaissance man. Born in 1875 in Scotland (where his novels are still as popular as those of Walter Scott), he wrote that "wood, sea, and hill were the intimacies of my childhood, and have never lost their spell for me." During his tenure as Governor General of Canada, from 1935 until his death in 1940, he climbed a cliff overlooking the Mackenzie River. Best known for his spy novel, *The Thirty-Nine Steps* (1915), Buchan was a member of the Alpine Club and contributed much to the literature of mountaineering, as shown by this excerpt from *The Last Secrets* (1923) describing the Italian Duke d'Abruzzi's 1906 expedition to map Uganda's mysterious Mountains of the Moon.

· · ·

IN APRIL, 1906, the Duke of the Abruzzi and his party left Italy to solve once and for all the riddle of the mountains. The Duke was perhaps the greatest of living mountaineers. As a rock-climber his fame has filled the Alps, and no name is more honoured at Courmayeur or the Montanvert. He had led polar expeditions, and had made the first ascent of the Alaskan Mount St. Elias. His experience, therefore, had made him not only a climber but an organizer of mountain travel. It was to this latter accomplishment that he owed his success, for Ruwenzori was not so much a climber's as a traveller's problem. The actual mountaineering is not hard, but to travel the long miles from Entebbe to the range, to cut a path through the dense jungles of the valleys, and to carry supplies and scientific apparatus to the high glacier camps, required an organizing talent of the first order.

The Duke left no contingency unforeseen. He took with him four celebrated Courmayeur guides, and a staff of distinguished scientists, as well as Cav. Vittorio Sella, the greatest of living mountain photographers. So large was the expedition that two hundred and fifty native porters were required to carry stores from Entebbe to Fort Portal. It was not a bold personal adventure, like Mr. Wollaston's, but a carefully planned, scientific assault upon the mystery of Ruwenzori. The Duke did not only seek to ascend the highest peak, but to climb every summit, and map accurately every mountain, valley, and glacier. The story of the work has been officially written, not indeed by the leader himself, who had no time to spare, but by his friend and former companion, Sir Filippo de Filippi. It is an admirable account, clear and yet picturesque, and it is illustrated by photographs and panoramas which have not often been equalled in mountaineering narratives.

The charm of the book is its strangeness. It tells of a kind of mountaineering to which the world can show no parallel. When Lhasa had been visited, Ruwenzori remained, with the gorges of the Brahmaputra, one of the few great geographical mysteries unveiled. Happily the unveiling has not killed the romance, for the truth is stranger than any forecast. If the Mountains of the Moon are lower than we had believed, they are far more wonderful. Here you have a range almost on the Equator, rising not from an upland, like Kilimanjaro, but from the "Albertine Depression," which is 600 or 700 feet below the average level of Uganda; a range of which the highest peaks are 1,000 feet higher than Mont Blanc, which is draped most days of the year in mist, and accessible from the plains only by deep-cut glens choked with strange trees and flowers. The altitude would in any case give every stage of climate from torrid to arctic, but the position on the Line adds something exotic even to familiar mountain sights, draping a glacier moraine with a tangle of monstrous growths, and swelling the homely alpine flora into portents. The freakish spirit in Nature has been let loose, and she has set snowfields and rock *arêtes* in the heart of a giant hothouse.

The Duke of the Abruzzi was faced at the start with a deplorable absence of information. Even the season when the weather was most favorable was disputed. Mr. Freshfield, following Sir Harry Johnston's advice, tried November, and found a perpetual shower-bath. Warned by this experience, the Duke selected June and July for the attempt, and was fortunate enough to get sufficient clear days to complete his task, though he was repeatedly driven into camp by violent rain. Another matter in doubt was the best means of approach to the highest snows. The obvious route was the Mobuku valley, but by this time it was pretty clear that Kiyanja, the peak at its head, was not the highest, and it was possible that there might be no way out of the valley to the higher western summits. Still, it had been the old way of travellers, and since the alternative was the Butagu valley right on the other side of the range, the Duke chose to follow the steps of his predecessors.

Just before Butiti he got his first sight of the snow, and made out that a double peak, which was certainly not Johnston's Duwoni, was clearly the loftiest. Duwoni came into view again in the lower Mobuku valley, and the sight, combined with the known locality of Kiyanja, enabled the expedition to take its bearings. Duwoni was seen through the opening of a large tributary valley, the Bujuku, which entered the Mobuku on the north side between the Portal Peaks. Now it had been clear from the lowlands that the highest snows were to the south of Duwoni, and must consequently lie between that peak and the Mobuku valley. The conclusion was that the Bujuku must lead to the foot of the highest summits, while the Mobuku could not. The discovery was the key of the whole geography of the range. But the Duke did not at once act upon it. He wisely decided to explore Kiyanja first; so, thinning out his caravan and leaving his heavier stores at the last native village, he with his party pushed up the Mobuku torrent.

The Mobuku valley falls in stages from the glacier, and at the foot of each stage is a cliff face and a waterfall. The soil everywhere oozes moisture, and where an outcrop of rock or a mat of dead boughs does not give firmer going, it is knee-deep in black mud. The first stage is forest land—great conifers with masses of ferns and tree-ferns below, and above a tangle of creepers and flaming orchids. At the second terrace you come to the fringe of alpine life. Here is the heath forest, of which let the narrative tell:

> Trunks and boughs are entirely smothered in a thick layer of mosses which hang like waving beards from every spray, cushion and englobe every knot, curl and swell around each twig, deform every outline and obliterate every feature, till the trees are a mere mass of grotesque contortions, monstrous tumefactions of the discoloured leprous growth. No leaf is to be seen save on the very topmost twigs, yet the forest is dark owing to the dense network of trunks and branches. The soil disappears altogether under innumerable dead trunks, heaped one upon another in intricate piles, covered with mosses, viscous and slippery when exposed to the air; black, naked, and yet neither mildewed nor rotten where they have lain for years and years in deep holes. No forest can be grimmer and stranger than this. The vegetation seems primeval, of some period when forms were uncertain and provisory.

But the third terrace is stranger still. There one is out of the forest and in an alpine meadow between sheer cliffs, with far at the head the gorge of Bujongolo and the tongue of the glacier above it. But what an alpine meadow!

> The ground was carpeted with a deep layer of lycopodium and springy moss, and thickly dotted with big clumps of the papery flowers, pink, yellow, and silver white, of the helichry-sum or everlasting, above which rose the tall columnar stalks of the lobelia, like funeral torches, beside huge branching groups of the monster senecio. The impression produced was beyond words to describe; the spectacle was too weird, too improbable, too unlike all familiar images, and upon the whole brooded the same grave deathly silence.

It is a comm3onplace to say that in savage Africa man is sur-rounded by a fauna still primeval; but in these mountains the flora, too, is of an earlier world—that strange world which is embalmed in our coal seams. Under the veil of mist, among cliffs which lose themselves in the clouds, the traveller walks in an unearthly landscape, which the gaunt candelabra of the sene-cios, the flambeaus of the lobelias, and the uncanny blooms of the helichryse like decorations at some ghostly feast. The word "helichryse" calls up ridiculous Theocritean associations, as if the sunburnt little "creeping gold" of Sicily were any kin to these African marvels! Our elders were wise when they named the range the Mountains of the Moon, for such things might well belong to some lunar gorge of Mr. Wells's imagination. Beyond Kiyanja the Duke found a little lake where a fire had raged and the senecios were charred and withered. It was a veritable Val-ley of Dry Bones.

Bujongolo offered the expedition a stone-heap overhung by a cliff, and there the permanent camp was fixed. Among mildews and lichens and pallid mist and an everlasting drip of rain five weeks were passed with this unpromising spot as their base. The first business was to ascend Kiyanja. This gave little trouble, for the ridge was soon gained, and an easy *arête* to the south led to the chief point. The height proved to be 15,988 feet, and the view from the summit settled the geography of the range and confirmed the Duke's theories. For it was now clear that the ridge at the head of the Mobuku was no part of the watershed of the chain, and that the Duwoni of Johnston was to the north, not of the Mobuku, but of the Bujuku. The highest summits stood over to the west, rising from the col at the head of the Bujuku valley. The Duke saw that they might also be reached by making a detour to the south of Kiyanja, and ascending a glen which is one of the high affluents of the Butagu, the great valley on the west side of the system.

It may be convenient here to explain the main features of the range, giving them the new names which the expedition invented, and which are now adopted by geographers. Kiyanja became Mount Baker, and its highest point is called Edward Peak after the then King of England. Due south, across the Freshfield Pass, stands Mount Luigi di Savoia, a name given by the Royal Geographical Society and not by the Duke, who wished to christen it after Joseph Thomson the traveller. Due north from Mount Baker, and separated from it by the upper Bujuku valley, is Mount Speke (the Duwoni of Johnston), with its main summit called Vittorio Emanuele. West of the gap between Baker and Speke stands the highest summit of all, Mount Stanley, with its twin peaks Margherita and Alexandra. North of Mount Speke is Mount Emin, and east of the latter is Mount Gessi. Five of the great *massifs* cluster around the Bujuku valley, while the sixth, Mount Luigi di Savoia, stands by itself at the south end of the chain.

The assault on Mount Stanley was delayed for some days by abominable weather. At last came a clear season, and the Duke with his guides crossed Freshfield Pass and ascended the valley at the back of Mount Baker. There they spent an evening, which showed what Ruwenzori could be like when clouds are absent. They found a little lake, embosomed in flowers, under the cliffs, and looking to the west they saw the sun set in crimson and gold over the great spaces of the Congo Forest. Next day they reached the col which bears the name of Scott Elliot, and encamped on one of the Mount Stanley glaciers at the height of 14,817 feet. At 7:30 on the following morning they reached the top of the first peak, Alexandra, 16,749 feet high. A short descent and a difficult piece of step-cutting through snow cornices took them to the summit of Margherita (16,815 feet), the highest point of the range:

> They emerged from the mist into splendid clear sunlight. At their feet lay a sea of fog. An impenetrable layer of light ashy-white cloud-drift, stretching as far as the eye could reach, was drifting rapidly north-westward. From the immense moving surface emerged two fixed points, two pure white peaks spar-

kling in the sun with their myriad snow crystals. These were the two extreme summits of the highest peaks. The Duke of the Abruzzi named these summits Margherita and Alexandra, "in order that, under the auspices of these two royal ladies, the memory of the two nations may be handed down to posterity—of Italy, whose name was the first to resound on these snows in a shout of victory, and of England, which in its marvellous colonial expansion carries civilization to the slopes of these remote mountains." It was a thrilling moment when the little tricolour flag, given by H.M. Queen Margherita of Savoy, unfurled to the wind and sun the embroidered letters of its inspiring motto, "Ardisci e Spera."

UP THE MÖRDERBERG

H.G. WELLS

Herbert George Wells (1866–1946) was trained as a biologist by T.H. Huxley, wrote *A Textbook of Biology* (1893), and then invented science fiction with *The Time Machine* (1895) and *The War of the Worlds* (1898). His mind was prodigious and incisive, and his writing, though always passionate, was often tinged with sardonic humor—of which this short story, in which a climber takes his aged mother up a difficult mountain, is a fine example. Wells was an ardent Fabian socialist, and part of the delight in this excerpt lies in its satirizing a sport that was seen as a pastime of the idle rich.

. . .

I MADE A KIND of record at Arosa by falling down three separate crevasses on three successive days. That was before little mother followed me out there. When she came, I could see at a glance she was tired and jaded and worried, and so, instead of letting her fret about in the hotel and get into a wearing tangle of gossip, I packed her and two knapsacks up, and started off on a long, refreshing, easy-going walk northward, until a blister on her foot stranded us at the Magenruhe Hotel on the Sneejoch. She was for going on, blister or no blister—I never met pluck like mother's in all my life—but I said "No. This is a mountaineering inn, and it suits me down to the ground—or if you prefer it, up to the sky. You shall sit on the veranda by the telescope, and I'll prance about among the peaks for a bit."

"Don't have accidents," she said.

"Can't promise that, little mother," I said; "but I'll always remember I'm your only son."

So I pranced . . .

I need hardly say that in a couple of days I was at loggerheads with all the mountaineers at that inn. They couldn't stand me. They didn't like my neck with its strong, fine Adam's apple—being mostly men with their heads *jammed* on—and they didn't like the way I bore myself and lifted my aviator's nose to the peaks. They didn't like my being a vegetarian and the way I evidently enjoyed it, and they didn't like the touch of colour, orange and green, in my rough serge suit. They were all of the dingy school—the sort of men I call gentlemanly owls— shy, correct-minded creatures, mostly from Oxford, and as solemn over their climbing as a cat frying eggs. Sage they were, great headnodders, and "I wouldn't-venture-to-do-a-thing-like-that"-ers. They always did what the books and guides advised, and they classed themselves by their seasons; one was in his ninth season, and another in his tenth, and so on. I was a novice and had to sit with my mouth open for bits of humble-pie.

My style that! Rather!

I would sit in the smoking-room sucking away at a pipeful of hygienic herb tobacco—they said it smelt like burning garden rubbish—and waiting to put my spoke in and let a little light into their minds. They set aside their natural reticence altogether in their efforts to show how much they didn't like me.

"You chaps take these blessed mountains too seriously," I said. "They're larks, and you've got to lark with them."

They just slued their eyes round at me.

"I don't find the solemn joy in fussing you do. The old-style mountaineers went up with alpenstocks and ladders and light hearts. That's my idea of mountaineering."

"It isn't ours," said one red-boiled hero of the peaks, all blisters and peeling skin, and he said it with an air of crushing me.

"It's the right idea," I said serenely, and puffed at my herb tobacco.

"When you've had a bit of experience you'll know better," said another, an oldish young man with a small grey beard.

"Experience never taught *me* anything," I said.

"Apparently not," said someone, and left me one down and me to play. I kept perfectly tranquil.

"I mean to do the Mörderberg before I go down," I said quietly, and produced a sensation.

"When are you going down?"

"Week or so," I answered, unperturbed.

"It's not the climb a man ought to attempt in his first year," said the peeling gentleman.

"*You* particularly ought not to try it," said another.

"No guide will go with you."

"Foolhardy idea."

"Mere brag."

"Like to see him do it."

I just let them boil for a bit, and when they were back to the simmer I dropped in, pensively, with "Very likely I'll take that little mother of mine. She's small, bless her, but she's as hard as nails."

But they saw they were being drawn by my ill-concealed smile; and this time they contented themselves with a few grunts and grunt-like remarks, and then broke up into little conversations in undertones that pointedly excluded me. It had the effect of hardening my purpose. I'm a stiff man when I'm put on my mettle, and I determined that the little mother *should* go up the Mörderberg, where half these solemn experts hadn't been, even if I had to be killed or orphaned in the attempt. So I spoke to her about it the next day. She was in a deck-chair on the veranda, wrapped up in rugs and looking at the peaks.

"Comfy?" I said.

"Very," she said.

"Getting rested?"

"It's so nice."

I strolled to the rail of the veranda. "See that peak there, mummy?"

She nodded happily, with eyes half shut.

"That's the Mörderberg. You and me have got to be up there the day after to-morrow."

Her eyes opened a bit. "Wouldn't it be rather a climb, dearest?" she asked.

"I'll manage that all right," I said, and she smiled consentingly and closed her eyes.

"So long as you manage it," she said.

I went down the valley that afternoon to Daxdam to get gear and guides and porters, and I spent the next day in glacier and rock practice above the hotel. That didn't add to my popularity. I made two little slips. One took me down a crevasse—I've an extraordinary knack of going down crevasses—and a party of three which was starting for the Kinderspitz spent an hour and a half fishing me out; and the other led to my dropping my ice-axe on a little string of people going for the Humpi glacier. It didn't go within thirty inches of anyone, but you might have thought from the row they made that I had knocked out the collective brains of the party. Quite frightful language they used, and three ladies with them, too!

The next day there was something very like an organized attempt to prevent our start. They brought out the landlord, they remonstrated with mother, they did their best to blacken the character of my two guides. The landlord's brother had a first-class row with them.

"Two years ago," he said, "they lost their Herr!"

"No particular reason," I said, "why you shouldn't keep yours on, is it?"

That settled him. He wasn't up to the polyglot pun, and it stuck in his mind like a fishbone in the throat.

Then the peeling gentleman came along and tried to overhaul our equipment. "Have you got this?" it was, and "Have you got that?"

"Two things," I said, looking at his nose pretty hard, "we haven't forgotten. One's blue veils and the other vaseline."

I've still a bright little memory of the start. There was the pass a couple of hundred feet or so below the hotel, and the hotel—all name and windows—standing out in a great, desolate, rocky place against lumpy masses of streaky green rock, flecked here and there with patches of snow and dark shelves of rhododendron, and rising perhaps a thousand feet towards the western spur of the massif. Our path ran before us, meandering among the boulders down to stepping-stones over a rivulet, and then upward on the other side of the stream towards the Magenruhe glacier, where we had to go up the rocks to the left and then across the icefall to shelves on the precipitous face on the west side. It was dawn, and the sun had still to rise, and everything looked very cold and blue and vast about us. Everyone in the hotel had turned out to bear a hand in the row—some of the *deshabilles* were disgraceful—and now they stood in a silent group watching us recede. The last word I caught was, "They'll have to come back."

"We'll come back all right," I answered. "Never fear."

And so we went on our way, cool and deliberate, over the stream and up and up towards the steep snowfields and icy shoulder of the Mörderberg. I remember that we went in absolute silence for a time, and then how suddenly the landscape gladdened with sunrise, and in an instant, as if speech had thawed, all our tongues were babbling.

I had one or two things in the baggage that I hadn't cared for the people at the inn to see, and I had made no effort to explain why I had five porters with the load of two and a half. But when we came to the icefall I showed my hand a little, and unslung a stout twine hammock for the mater. We put her in this with a rug round her, and sewed her in with a few stitches; then we roped up in line, with me last but one and a guide front and rear, and mummy in the middle carried by two of the porters. I struck my alpenstock through two holes I had made in the shoulders of my jacket under my rucksac, T-shape to my body, so that when I went down a crevasse, as I did ever and again, I just stuck in its jaws and came up easy as the rope grew taut. And so, except for one or two bumps that made the mater chuckle, we got over without misadventure.

Then came the rock climb on the other side, requiring much judgment. We had to get from ledge to ledge as opportunity offered, and there the little mother was a perfect godsend. We unpacked her after we had slung her over the big fissure—I forget what you call it—that always comes between glacier and rock—and whenever we came to a bit of ledge within eight feet of the one we were working along, the two guides took her and slung her up, she being so light, and then she was able to give a foot for the next man to hold by and hoist himself. She said we were all pulling her leg, and that made her and me laugh so much that the whole party had to wait for us.

It was pretty tiring altogether doing that bit of the climb—two hours we had of it before we got to the loose masses of rock on the top of the arete. "It's worse going down," said the elder guide.

I looked back for the first time, and I confess it did make me feel a bit giddy. There was the glacier looking quite pretty, and with a black gash between itself and the rocks.

For a time it was pretty fair going up the rocky edge of the arete, and nothing happened of any importance, except that one of the porters took to grousing because he was hit on the shin by a stone I dislodged. "Fortunes of war," I said, but he didn't seem to see it, and when I just missed him with a second he broke out into a long, whining discourse in what I suppose he thought was German—*I* couldn't make head or tail of it.

"He says you might have killed him," said the little mother.

"They say," I quoted, "What say they? *Let* them say."

I was for stopping and filling him up with a feed, but the elder guide wouldn't have it. We had already lost time, he said, and the traverse round the other face of the mountain would be more and more subject to avalanches as the sun got up. So we went on. As we went round the corner to the other face I turned towards the hotel—it was the meanest little oblong spot by now—and made a derisive gesture or so for the benefit of anyone at the telescope.

We did get one rock avalanche that reduced the hindmost guide to audible prayer, but nothing hit us except a few bits of snow. The rest of the fall was a couple of yards and more out from us. We were on rock just then and overhung; before and afterwards we were edging along steps in an ice-slope cut by the foremost guide, and touched up by the porters. The avalanche was much more impressive before it came in sight, banging and thundering overhead, and it made a tremendous uproar in the blue deeps beneath, but in actual transit it seemed a mean show—mostly of stones smaller than I am.

"All right?" asked the guide.

"Toned up," I answered.

"I suppose it *is* safe, dear?" asked the little mother.

"Safe as Trafalgar Square," I said. "Hop along, mummykins."

Which she did with remarkable agility.

The traverse took us on to old snow at last, and here we could rest for lunch—and pretty glad we were both of lunch and rest. But here the trouble with the guides and porters thickened. They were already a little ruffled about my animating way with loose rocks, and now they kicked up a tremendous shindy because instead of the customary brandy we had brought non-alcoholic ginger cordial. Would they even try it? Not a bit of it! It was a queer little dispute, high up in that rarefied air, about food values and the advantages of making sandwiches with nuttar. They were an odd lot of men, invincibly set upon a vitiated and vitiating dietary. They wanted meat, they wanted alcohol, they wanted narcotics to smoke. You might have thought that men like these, living in almost direct contact with nature, would have liked "nature" foods, such as plasmon, protose, plobose, digestine, and so forth. Not them! They just craved for corruption. When I spoke of drinking pure water one of the porters spat in a marked, symbolic manner over the precipice. From that point onward discontent prevailed.

We started again about half-past eleven, after a vain attempt on the part of the head guide to induce us to turn back. We had

now come to what is generally the most difficult part of the Mörderberg ascent, the edge that leads up to the snowfield below
the crest. But here we came suddenly into a draught of warm
air blowing from the south-west, and everything, the guide said,
was unusual. Usually the edge is a sheet of ice over rock. To-day
it was wet and soft, and one could kick steps in it and get one's
toes into rock with the utmost ease.

"This is where Herr Tomlinson's party fell," said one of the
porters, after we'd committed ourselves to the edge for ten minutes or so.

"Some people could fall out of a four-post bed," I said.

"It'll freeze hard again before we come back," said the second
guide, "and us with nothing but verdammt ginger inside of us."

"You keep your rope taut," said I.

A friendly ledge came to the help of mother in the nick of
time, just as she was beginning to tire, and we sewed her up all
but the feet in her hammock again, and roped her carefully. She
bumped a bit, and at times she was just hanging over immen-
sity and rotating slowly, with everybody else holding on like
grim death.

"My dear," she said, the first time this happened, "is it *right*
for me to be doing this?"

"Quite right," I said, "but if you can get a foothold presently
again—it's rather better style."

"You're sure there's no danger, dear?"

"Not a scrap."

"And I don't fatigue you?"

"You're a stimulant."

"The view," she said, "is certainly becoming very beautiful."

But presently the view blotted itself out, and we were in clouds and a thin drift of almost thawing snowflakes.

We reached the upper snowfield about half-past one, and the snow was extraordinarily soft. The elder guide went in up to his armpits.

"Frog it," I said, and spread myself out flat, in a sort of swimming attitude. So we bored our way up to the crest and along it. We went in little spurts and then stopped for breath, and we dragged the little mother after us in her hammock-bag. Sometimes the snow was so good we fairly skimmed the surface; sometimes it was so rotten we plunged right into it and splashed about. I went too near the snow cornice once and it broke under me, but the rope saved me, and we reached the summit about three o'clock without further misadventure. The summit was just bare rock with the usual cairn and pole. Nothing to make a fuss about. The drift of snow and cloudwisp had passed, the sun was blazing hot overhead, and we seemed to be surveying all Switzerland. The Magenruhe Hotel was at our toes, hidden, so to speak, by our chins. We squatted about the cairn, and the guides and porters were reduced to ginger and vegetarian ham-sandwiches. I cut and scratched an inscription, saying I had climbed on simple food, and claiming a record.

Seen from the summit the snowfields on the north-east side of the mountain looked extremely attractive, and I asked the head guide why that way up wasn't used. He said something in his peculiar German about precipices.

So far our ascent had been a fairly correct ascent in rather slow time. It was in the descent that the strain in me of almost unpremeditated originality had play. I wouldn't have the rope returning across the upper snowfield, because mother's hands and feet were cold, and I wanted her to jump about a bit. And before I could do anything to prevent it she had slipped, tried to get up by rolling over *down* the slope instead of up, as she ought to have done, and was leading the way, rolling over and over and over, down towards the guide's blessed precipices above the lower snowfield.

I didn't lose an instant in flinging myself after her, axe up, in glissading attitude. I'm not clear what I meant to do, but I fancy the idea was to get in front of her and put on the brake. I did not succeed, anyhow. In twenty seconds I had slipped, and was sitting down and going down out of my own control altogether.

Now, most great discoveries are the result of accident, and I maintain that in that instant mother and I discovered two distinct and novel ways of coming down a mountain.

It is necessary that there should be first a snow slope above with a layer of softish, rotten snow on the top of ice, then a precipice, with a snow-covered talus sloping steeply at first and then less steeply, then more snow slopes and precipices according to taste, ending in a snowfield or a not-too-greatly-fissured glacier, or a reasonable, not-too-rocky slope. Then it all becomes as easy as chuting the chutes.

Mother hit on the sideways method. She rolled. With the snow in the adhesive state it had got into she had made the jolliest little snowball of herself in half a minute, and the nucleus of as clean and abundant a snow avalanche as anyone could wish. There was plenty of snow going in front of her, and that's the very essence of both our methods. You must fall on your snow, not your snow on you, or it smashes you. And you mustn't mix yourself up with loose stones.

I, on the other hand, went down feet first, and rather like a snow-plough; slower than she did, and if, perhaps, with less charm, with more dignity. Also I saw more. But it was certainly a tremendous rush. And I gave a sort of gulp when mummy bumped over the edge into the empty air and vanished.

It was like a toboggan ride gone mad down the slope until I took off from the edge of the precipice, and then it was like a dream.

I'd always thought falling must be horrible. It wasn't in the slightest degree. I might have hung with my clouds and lumps of snow about me for weeks, so great was my serenity. I had an impression then that I was as good as killed—and that it didn't matter. I wasn't afraid—that's nothing!—but I wasn't a bit uncomfortable. Whack! We'd hit something, and I expected to be flying to bits right and left. But we'd only got onto the snow-slope below, at so steep an angle that it was merely breaking the fall. Down we went again. I didn't see much of the view after that because the snow was all round and over my head, but I kept feet foremost and in a kind of sitting posture, and then I slowed and then I quickened again and bumped rather, and then harder, and bumped and then bumped again and came to rest. This time I was altogether buried in snow, and twisted sideways with a lot of heavy snow on my right shoulder.

I sat for a bit enjoying the stillness—and then I wondered what had become of mother, and set myself to get out of the snow about me. It wasn't so easy as you might think; the stuff was all in lumps and spaces like a gigantic sponge, and I lost my temper and struggled and swore a good deal, but at last I managed it. I crawled out and found myself on the edge of heaped masses of snow quite close to the upper part of the Magenruhe glacier. And far away, right up the glacier and near the other side, was a little thing like a black-beetle struggling in the heart of an immense split ball of snow.

I put my hands to my mouth and let out with my version of the yodel, and presently I saw her waving her hand.

It took me nearly twenty minutes to get to her. I knew my weakness, and I was very careful of every crevasse I came near. When I got up to her her face was anxious.

"What have you done with the guides?" she asked.

"They've got too much to carry," I said. "They're coming down another way. Did you like it?"

"Not very much, dear," she said; "but I dare say I shall get used to these things. Which way do we go now?"

I decided we'd find a snow-bridge across the bergschrund—that's the word I forgot just now—and so get on to the rocks on the east side of the glacier, and after that we had uneventful going right down to the hotel...

OUR RETURN EVOKED such a strain of hostility and envy as I have never met before or since. First they tried to make out we'd never been to the top at all, but mother's little proud voice settled that sort of insult. And, besides, there was the evidence of the guides and porters following us down. When they asked about the guides, "They're following *your* methods," I said, "and I suppose they'll get back here to-morrow morning some-when."

That didn't please them.

I claimed a record. They said my methods were illegitimate.

"If I see fit," I said, "to use an avalanche to get back by, what's that to you? You tell me me and mother can't do the confounded mountain anyhow, and when we do you want to invent a lot of rules to disqualify us. You'll say next one mustn't glissade. I've made a record, and you know I've made a record, and you're about as sour as you can be. The fact of it is, you chaps don't know your own silly business. Here's a good, quick way of coming down a mountain, and you ought to know about it—"

"The chance that both of you are not killed was one in a thousand."

"Nonsense! It's the proper way to come down for anyone who hasn't a hide-bound mind. You chaps ought to practise falling great heights in snow. It's perfectly easy and perfectly safe, if only you know how to set about it."

"Look here, young man," said the oldish young man with the little grey beard, "you don't seem to understand that you and that lady have been saved by a kind of miracle—"

"Theory!" I interrupted. "I'm surprised you fellows ever come to Switzerland. If I were your kind I'd just invent theoretical mountains and play for points. However, you're tired, little mummy. It's time you had some nice warm soup and tucked yourself up in bed. I shan't let you up for six-and-thirty hours."

But it's queer how people detest a little originality.

THE CREATION OF THE
NORTHERN
ROCKY MOUNTAINS

DOGRIB NATION

The Dogrib are a nation of Northern Cree or Dene whose traditional homeland lay between Great Bear and Great Slave lakes, in what is now Canada's Northwest Territories, and who migrated annually to the north to hunt caribou. They have a number of creation myths explaining the origins of the physical landscape they inhabited, including the Rocky Mountains. Several characters recur, among them the Mackenzie River, which is called Too-cha-tes, meaning Big Water; and Big Man, Naba-Cha, the Dogrib name for a stream that joins the Mackenzie near its mouth at the Arctic Ocean. The following story was recorded in 1903 by James M. Bell and published in the *Journal of American Folklore*.

. . .

THE BIG MAN, Naba-Cha, was one of the very largest men who ever lived. The lodge which was his home was made of three hundred skins of the biggest caribou that could be killed on the plains that lie north of his river. The dish from which he

ate his meals was made of the bark of six huge birch trees. And
it took one whole moose, or two caribou, or fifty partridges to
feed him every day.

Big Man was known throughout the whole North Country,
for he had often made war against the tribes to the north, the
east, and the south. Northward he had travelled to the mouth
of Big Water to fight the Snow Men, the Eskimoes. Eastward,
he had crossed Great Bear Lake to the country of the Yellow-
knives. There he had seen the pure copper shining in the sands
of the rivers that flow toward Great Bear Lake and Great Slave
Lake and toward the icy ocean.

Southward, he had travelled a long distance to the great
plains, the country of the Crees, where he had seen many large
animals. But westward he had never gone, because there lived a
giant man, a man bigger than Naba-Cha.

Naba-Cha was not only big; he was wicked and very cruel.
He was especially cruel to a Cree boy he had brought back from
the south one time when he was on the war-path. The boy was
an orphan, without father or mother, sister or brother, to help
him escape. His name was Caribou-footed.

The boy had one friend in the lodge of Big Man. That was
Hottah, the two-year-old moose, the cleverest of all the northern animals. Swift he was, too. He had travelled, in one day, all
the long distance from the mouth of Big Water to the home of
Big Man.

Hottah liked Caribou-footed so much that he wanted to help
him escape from Big Man. He knew that far to the westward,

much farther west than Big Man had ever gone, flowed another river almost as long and wide as Big Water. The Yukon, it is called. West of the Yukon, he knew, lay safety for Caribou-footed. There lived Nesnabi, the Good Man.

So one day Hottah said to the boy, "We will go away. You take a stone, a clod of earth, a piece of moss, and a branch of a tree. Together we shall escape from the cruel Big Man. I will carry you on my back."

Caribou-footed gathered the things he was told to get, and soon the two were ready to leave. Hottah took the boy upon his back and carried him out to the great plains west of Big Water. But before long they saw Big Man coming behind them, riding his great caribou.

"Fling out behind you your clod of earth," said Hottah to the boy.

Caribou-footed did so, and at once there rose behind them, between them and Big Man, great hills of earth. The hills were so high and wide that it was many days before Big Man came in sight again. During those days Hottah chewed the sweet grass that grew west of the hills, and Caribou-footed ate the ripe berries.

When Big Man came in sight a second time, Hottah called to the boy, "Fling out behind you your piece of moss."

Caribou-footed did so, and at once a vast muskeg-swamp lay behind them. For days the caribou and Big Man floundered in the muskeg, while Hottah and the boy moved on toward the setting sun. When Big Man appeared a third time, Hottah said to the boy, "Fling behind you your stone."

Caribou-footed did so, and at once there rose behind them, between them and Big Man, high rocky mountains. Up to the clouds they rose, white with snow, more magnificent than had ever been seen before. It was a long time before Big Man and his caribou had crossed the mountains and appeared again to Hottah and the boy. Then they were much nearer their goal, the great western river.

"Now fling out behind you your branch of a tree."

Caribou-footed did so, and at once arose a mighty forest, with trees so thick that Big Man and his gigantic caribou could not pass between them. Big Man had to cut his way through. And because its horns had stuck in the branches, the caribou was left behind.

By the time Big Man came in sight again, Hottah had carried the boy safely across the great river, the Yukon. Away toward the west it wound, through high rocky hills, foaming as it flowed.

Big Man reached the bank of the river and, seeing Hottah on the other side, called to him, "Help me, Hottah. Help me cross this turbulent river. If you will assist me to the country that lies beyond, I will do no harm to the boy. I promise you."

Without a word Hottah went to get Big Man. But as they were crossing the great river, Hottah dropped the giant into the water. Down he was swept by the swirling rapids of the river, on and on toward the setting sun.

Thus the wicked and cruel Bad Man, Naba-Cha, was lost forever, and thus Caribou-footed was saved. And in the far Northwest, the foothills, the muskeg-swamp, the snow-capped

Rocky Mountains, and the great forest remain where the Cree boy threw the clod of earth, the piece of moss, the stone, and the branch of a tree, long, long ago.

THE CONQUEST
OF MOUNT McKINLEY

BELMORE BROWNE

A naturalist, writer, and one of America's best-known landscape artists, Browne was born in New York in 1880, studied at the Académie Julian in Paris, and traveled to Alaska in his capacity as specimen collector for the American Museum of Natural History in the early 1900s. Fascinated with Alaska's rugged mountains, he became obsessed with the idea of climbing Mount McKinley (now Denali), the continent's highest, most inaccessible mountain. He made three attempts—in 1906, 1910, and 1912—but, as he recounts in this excerpt from his book, *The Conquest of Mount McKinley* (1913), was stormed off only 125 feet from the summit. He died in 1954, but his name lives on in his paintings and in Belmore Browne Peak, in Alberta's Kananaskis Provincial Park.

. . .

IT WAS THE EVENING of July 6th. Professor Parker was resting inside the big tent. La Voy, Aten, and I had been drying and airing our mountain tent and duffle and doing odd jobs around camp. The sky was a sickly green colour, and the air seemed heavy and lifeless. After finishing our work we rested in the heather and talked of our plans for our coming journey to the Yukon.

The sky reminded me of sinister skies that I had seen on the eastern seacoast before heavy storms, and I turned to Aten and said that were I on a boat I would overhaul the ground tackle and see that everything was snug because it looked like "dirty weather." The words were scarcely out of my mouth before a deep rumbling came from the Alaskan Range. I can only compare the sound to thunder, but it had a deep hollow quality that was unlike thunder, a sinister suggestion of overwhelming power that was terrifying. I remember that as I looked, the Alaskan Range melted into mist and that the mountains were bellowing, and that Aten was yelling something I could not understand and that the valley above us turned white—and then the earth began to heave and roll, and I forgot everything but the desire to stay upright. In front of me was a boulder weighing about two hundred pounds. We had pulled it there with a sled and dog team to anchor our tent; it had sunk into the moss from its own weight, and as I watched, the boulder turned, broke loose from the earth, and moved several feet.

Then came the crash of our falling caches, followed by another muffled crash as the front of our hill slid into the creek, and a lake near by boiled as if it was hot.

The mossy surfaces of the hills were opening all about us, and as the surface opened the cracks filled with liquid mud, and then suddenly everything was still. We stood up dazed and looked about. The Alaskan Range was still wrapped in a haze of avalanche dust, and the country far and near was scarred, and stripped of vegetation where the earth had slid. Our dogs had fled at the beginning of the quake and we could hear them whimpering and running about through the willows.

Aten, with his pocket full of tobacco, was asking me impatiently for mine—and then we began to laugh. We ran to the tent to see how Professor Parker had fared, and then we howled again, for as we pulled the flaps aside it seemed as if everything that was movable, including the stove, had fallen in a heap. The stove had overturned and a great flat rock which we used as a base for the stove had moved towards the tent door.

While we were restoring order out of chaos, Aten, who was standing by the tent door, exclaimed: "Good God! Look at Brooks!" As we dashed out of the tent an awe-inspiring sight met our eyes. Just east of Mount McKinley stood a magnificent 12,000-foot peak. It was somewhat like the Matterhorn in shape, and formed the culminating pinnacle in a range some six miles in length that formed the eastern wall of the main eastern fork of the Muldrow Glacier. As this mountain was the finest peak east of Mount McKinley we were anxious to give it a worthy name and we decided to name it after Alfred Brooks, who had led the first survey party through this part of Alaska. While we were uncertain as to whether or not Brooks's name had already been attached to some other Alaskan mountain, we always spoke of the great peak as Mount Brooks. Now, as we reached the open and turned our eyes towards the mountain, we saw that the whole extent of the mountain wall that formed its western flank was avalanching. I have never seen a sight of such overpowering grandeur. The avalanche seemed to stretch along the range for a distance of several miles, like a huge wave, and like a huge wave it seemed to poise for an instant before it plunged downward onto the ice-fields thousands of feet below. The mountain was about ten miles away and we waited breathlessly until the terrific thunder of the falling mass began to boom and rumble among the mountains.

Following the inspiring salvos of nature's artillery came the aftermath we had learned to look for. Beyond the range that rimmed our valley a great white cloud began to rise. As it came into view and began to obscure the Brooks range we could almost check off its growth as it billowed upward with startling rapidity, two—three—four thousand feet until it hung like a huge opaque wall against the main range, and then it fell—the range that rimmed our valley was blotted out and the great wave of avalanche débris came rushing down our valley. We were already at work, strengthening our tent in frantic haste.

We knew that the cloud was advancing at a rate close to sixty miles an hour and that we did not have much time to spare. But with boulders to hold the bottom and tautened guy-ropes, we made the tent as solid as possible and got inside before the cloud struck us. The tent held fast, but after the "wullies" passed, the ground was spangled with ice-dust that only a few minutes before had formed the icy covering of a peak ten miles away!

Before we rolled up in our sleeping-bags, we took a last look about us. In every direction the earth and mountains were seamed and scarred and a great dun-coloured cloud of ice- and rock-dust hid the Alaskan Range. The streams, too, were flooding their banks, and ran chocolate-coloured from the earthslides that had dammed them. As we compared our adventures and sensations, we thought of the band of fifty caribou that we had seen in the head of the valley—what a sight they must have presented when the earthquake struck them! Fifty wild beasts plunging, falling, and wild-eyed with terror—I would give much to have been on a hillside nearby!

The earthquakes continued at regular intervals for about thirty-six hours. None of them could compare in strength with the first shock but many of them were severe enough to wreck a modern city. Strangely enough most of the shocks were preceded by a deep detonation. The sound resembled the noise made by exploding steam, and it came always from the same place—Mount McKinley. Experts on seismic disturbances have told me that the sound does not precede the disturbance, but in our case the reverse was true. We would be sitting in our tent, when suddenly the deep, explosive noise would reach our ears. One of us would say, "Here comes another," and if the explosion was of sufficient power we would take the precaution of seeing that our teapot was in a safe place. And then, after a few seconds had elapsed, the quake would reach us. After going through such an experience as the big quake, one realises, for the first time, the gigantic power of the forces of nature, and understands with what ease great mountain ranges have been formed.

My strongest impression immediately after the quake was one of surprise at the elasticity of the earth. We speak of being on "solid ground," but while the earthquake was occurring one felt as if the earth's crust was a quivering mass of jelly.

DAVID

EARLE BIRNEY

Born in Calgary, Alberta, in 1904, and raised in Banff, Earle Birney knew and loved the Rockies. His first book of poetry, *David and Other Poems*, appeared in 1942 and won the Governor General's Award. A stark but haunting narrative about a young man who falls from a mountain, as told by his companion, "David" is one of the best known poems in Canadian literature. The mountain Birney had in mind was Mount Louis, near Banff, and the narrator, Birney wrote, "is me at nineteen when I was romantic as hell." Romanticized or not, the poem perfectly captures the sharp, majestic beauty of the mountains and the fragility of the humans who move among them.

· · ·

I

David and I that summer cut trails on the survey,
All week in the valley for wages, in air that was steeped
In the wail of mosquitoes, but over the sunalive week-ends
We climbed, to get from the ruck of the camp, the surly

Poker, the wrangling, the snoring under the fetid
Tents, and because we had joy in our lengthening coltish
Muscles, and mountains for David were made to see over,
Stairs from the valleys and steps to the sun's retreats.

II
Our first was Mount Gleam. We hiked in the long afternoon
To a curling lake and lost the lure of the faceted
Cone in the swell of its sprawling shoulders. Past
The inlet we grilled our bacon, the strips festooned

On a poplar prong, in the hurrying slant of the sunset.
Then the two of us rolled in the blanket while round us the cold
Pines thrust at the stars. The dawn was a floating
Of mists till we reached to the slopes above timber, and won

To snow like fire in the sunlight. The peak was upthrust
Like a fist in a frozen ocean of rock that swirled
Into valleys the moon could be rolled in. Remotely unfurling
Eastward the alien prairie glittered. Down through the dusty

Skree on the west we descended, and David showed me
How to use the give of shale for giant incredible
Strides. I remember, before the larches' edge,
That I jumped on a long green surf of juniper flowing

Away from the wind, and landed in gentian and saxifrage
Spilled on the moss. Then the darkening firs
And the sudden whirring of water that knifed down a fern-hidden
Cliff and splashed unseen into mist in the shadows.

III

One Sunday on Rampart's arête a rainsquall caught us,
And passed, and we clung by our blueing fingers and bootnails
An endless hour in the sun, not daring to move
Till the ice had steamed from the slate. And David taught me

How time on a knife-edge can pass with the guessing
        of fragments
Remembered from poets, the naming of strata beside one,
And matching of stories from schooldays. . .We crawled astride
The peak to feast on the marching ranges flagged

By the fading shreds of the shattered stormcloud. Lingering
There it was David who spied to the south, remote,
And unmapped, a sunlit spire on Sawback, an overhang
Crooked like a talon. David named it the Finger.

That day we chanced on the skull and the splayed white ribs
Of a mountain goat underneath a cliff-face, caught
On a rock. Around were the silken feathers of hawks.
And that was the first I knew that a goat could slip.

IV

And then Inglismaldie. Now I remember only
The long ascent of the lonely valley, the live
Pine spirally scarred by lightning, the slicing pipe
Of invisible pika, and great prints, by the lowest

Snow, of a grizzly. There it was too that David
Taught me to read the scroll of coral in limestone

And the beetle-seal in the shale of ghostly trilobites,
Letters delivered to man from the Cambrian waves.

V

On Sundance we tried from the col and the going was hard.
The air howled from our feet to the smudged rocks
And the papery lake below. At an outthrust we balked
Till David clung with his left to a dint in the scarp,

Lobbed the iceaxe over the rocky lip,
Slipped from his holds and hung by the quivering pick,
Twisted his long legs up into space and kicked
To the crest. Then, grinning, he reached with his freckled wrist

And drew me up after. We set a new time for that climb.
That day returning we found a robin gyrating
In grass, wing-broken. I caught it to tame but David
Took and killed it, and said, "Could you teach it to fly?"

VI

In August, the second attempt, we ascended The Fortress,
By the forks of the Spray we caught five trout and fried them
Over a balsam fire. The woods were alive
With the vaulting of mule-deer and drenched with clouds
    all the morning,

Till we burst at noon to the flashing and floating round
Of the peaks. Coming down we picked in our hats the bright

And sunhot raspberries, eating them under a mighty
Spruce, while a marten moving like quicksilver scouted us.

VII

But always we talked of the Finger on Sawback, unknown
And hooked, till the first afternoon in September we slogged
Through the musky woods, past a swamp that quivered with
    frog-song,
And camped by a bottle-green lake. But under the cold

Breath of the glacier sleep would not come, the moon-light
Etching the Finger. We rose and trod past the feathery
Larch, while the stars went out, and the quiet heather
Flushed, and the skyline pulsed with the surging bloom

Of incredible dawn in the Rockies. David spotted
Bighorns across the moraine and sent them leaping
With yodels the ramparts redoubled and rolled to the peaks,
And the peaks to the sun. The ice in the morning thaw

Was a gurgling world of crystal and cold blue chasms,
And seracs that shone like frozen saltgreen waves.
At the base of the Finger we tried once and failed. Then David
Edged to the west and discovered the chimney; the last

Hundred feet we fought the rock and shouldered and kneed
Our way for an hour and made it. Unroping we formed
A cairn on the rotting tip. Then I turned to look north
At the glistening wedge of giant Assiniboine, heedless

Of handhold. And one foot gave. I swayed and shouted.
David turned sharp and reached out his arm and steadied me,
Turning again with a grin and his lips ready
To jest. But the strain crumbled his foothold. Without

A gasp he was gone. I froze to the sound of grating
Edge-nails and fingers, the slither of stones, the lone
Second of silence, the nightmare thud. Then only
The wind and the muted beat of unknowing cascades.

VIII
Somehow I worked down the fifty impossible feet
To the ledge, calling and getting no answer but echoes
Released in the cirque, and trying not to reflect
What an answer would mean. He lay still, with his lean

Young face upturned and strangely unmarred, but his legs
Splayed beneath him, beside the final drop,
Six hundred feet sheer to the ice. My throat stopped
When I reached him, for he was alive. He opened his grey

Straight eyes and brokenly murmured, "Over. . . over."
And I, feeling beneath him a cruel fang
Of the ledge thrust in his back, but not understanding,
Mumbled stupidly, "Best not to move," and spoke

Of his pain. But he said, "I can't move. . . If only I felt
Some pain." Then my shame stung the tears to my eyes
As I crouched, and I cursed myself, but he cried,
Louder, "No, Bobbie! Don't ever blame yourself.

I didn't test my foothold." He shut the lids
Of his eyes to the stare of the sky, while I moistened his lips
From our water flask and tearing my shirt into strips
I swabbed the shredded hands. But the blood slid

From his side and stained the stone and the thirsting lichens,
And yet I dared not lift him up from the gore
Of the rock. Then he whispered, "Bob, I want to go over!"
This time I knew what he meant and I grasped for a lie

And said, "I'll be back here by midnight with ropes
And men from the camp and we'll cradle you out." But I knew
That the day and the night must pass and the cold dews
Of another morning before such men unknowing

The ways of mountains could win to the chimney's top.
And then, how long? And he knew . . . and the hell of hours
After that, if he lived till we came, roping him out.
But I curled beside him and whispered, "The bleeding will stop.

You can last." He said only, "Perhaps . . . For what?
    A wheelchair,
Bob?" His eyes brightening with fever upbraided me.
I could not look at him more and said, "Then I'll stay
With you." But he did not speak, for the clouding fever.

I lay dazed and stared at the long valley,
The glistening hair of a creek on the rug stretched
By the firs, while the sun leaned round and flooded the ledge,
The moss, and David still as a broken doll.

I hunched to my knees to leave, but he called and his voice
Now was sharpened with fear. "For Christ's sake push me over!
If I could move . . . or die . . ." The sweat ran from his forehead
But only his head moved. A hawk was buoying

Blackly its wings over the wrinkled ice.
The purr of a waterfall rose and sank with the wind.
Above us climbed the last joint of the Finger
Beckoning bleakly the wide indifferent sky.

Even then in the sun it grew cold lying there . . . And I knew
He had tested his holds. It was I who had not . . . I looked
At the blood on the ledge, and the far valley. I looked
At last in his eyes. He breathed, "I'd do it for you, Bob."

IX
I will not remember how nor why I could twist
Up the wind-devilled peak, and down through the
 chimney's empty
Horror, and over the traverse alone. I remember
Only the pounding fear I would stumble on It

When I came to the grave-cold maw of the bergschrund . . .
 reeling
Over the sun-cankered snowbridge, shying the caves
In the névé . . . the fear, and the need to make sure It was there
On the ice, the running and falling and running, leaping

Of gaping greenthroated crevasses, alone and pursued
By the Finger's lengthening shadow. At last through the fanged

And blinding seracs I slid to the milky wrangling
Falls at the glacier's snout, through the rocks piled huge

On the humped moraine, and into the spectral larches,
Alone. By the glooming lake I sank and chilled
My mouth but I could not rest and stumbled still
To the valley, losing my way in the ragged marsh.

I was glad of the mire that covered the stains, on my ripped
Boots, of his blood, but panic was on me, the reek
Of the bog, the purple glimmer of toadstools obscene
In the twilight. I staggered clear to a firewaste, tripped

And fell with a shriek on my shoulder. It somehow eased
My heart to know I was hurt, but I did not faint
And I could not stop while over me hung the range
Of the Sawback. In blackness I searched for the trail by
    the creek

And found it . . . My feet squelched a slug and horror
Rose again in my nostrils. I hurled myself
Down the path. In the woods behind some animal yelped.
Then I saw the glimmer of tents and babbled my story.

I said that he fell straight to the ice where they found him,
And none but the sun and incurious clouds have lingered
Around the marks of that day on the ledge of the Finger,
That day, the last of my youth, on the last of our mountains.

THINKING

LIKE A MOUNTAIN

ALDO LEOPOLD

Born in Iowa in 1887, Aldo Leopold was a lifelong celebrant of the simple joys of a life lived in harmony with wilderness. He joined the U.S. Forest Service in 1909, became associate director of its Forest Products Laboratory in Madison, Wisconsin, in 1924, and in 1933 occupied the chair of game management at the University of Wisconsin—a position created especially for him. His book, *A Sand County Almanac and Sketches Here and There,* from which this essay is taken, was published in 1949, a year after Leopold's death (while fighting a ground fire on a neighbor's property). "There are some who can live without wild things, and some who cannot," he'd written in the foreword. Leopold was one who could not.

· · ·

A DEEP CHESTY bawl echoes from rimrock to rimrock, rolls down the mountain, and fades into the far blackness of the night. It is an outburst of wild defiant sorrow, and of contempt for all the adversities of the world.

Every living thing (and perhaps many a dead one as well) pays heed to that call. To the deer it is a reminder of the way of all flesh, to the pine a forecast of midnight scuffles and of blood upon the snow, to the coyote a promise of gleanings to come, to the cowman a threat of red ink at the bank, to the hunter a challenge of fang against bullet. Yet behind these obvious and immediate hopes and fears there lies a deeper meaning, known only to the mountain itself. Only the mountain has lived long enough to listen objectively to the howl of a wolf.

Those unable to decipher the hidden meaning know nevertheless that it is there, for it is felt in all wolf country, and distinguishes that country from all other land. It tingles in the spine of all who hear wolves by night, or who scan their tracks by day. Even without sight or sound of wolf, it is implicit in a hundred small events: the midnight whinny of a pack horse, the rattle of rolling rocks, the bound of a fleeing deer, the way shadows lie under the spruces. Only the ineducable tyro can fail to sense the presence or absence of wolves, or the fact that mountains have a secret opinion about them.

My own conviction on this score dates from the day I saw a wolf die. We were eating lunch on a high rimrock, at the foot of which a turbulent river elbowed its way. We saw what we thought was a doe fording the torrent, her breast awash in white water. When she climbed the bank toward us and shook out her tail, we realized our error: it was a wolf. A half-dozen others, evidently grown pups, sprang from the willows and all joined in a welcoming mêlée of wagging tails and playful maulings. What was literally a pile of wolves writhed and tumbled in the center of an open flat at the foot of our rimrock.

In those days we had never heard of passing up a chance to kill a wolf. In a second we were pumping lead into the pack, but with more excitement than accuracy: how to aim a steep down-hill shot is always confusing. When our rifles were empty, the old wolf was down, and a pup was dragging a leg into impass-able slide-rocks.

We reached the old wolf in time to watch a fierce green fire dying in her eyes. I realized then, and have known ever since, that there was something new to me in those eyes—something known only to her and to the mountain. I was young then, and full of trigger-itch; I thought that because fewer wolves meant more deer, that no wolves would mean hunters' paradise. But after seeing the green fire die, I sensed that neither the wolf nor the mountain agreed with such a view.

SINCE THEN I have lived to see state after state extirpate its wolves. I have watched the face of many a newly wolfless moun-tain, and seen the south-facing slopes wrinkle with a maze of new deer trails. I have seen every edible bush and seedling browsed, first to anaemic desuetude, and then to death. I have seen every edible tree defoliated to the height of a saddlehorn. Such a mountain looks as if someone had given God a new prun-ing shears, and forbidden Him all other exercise. In the end the starved bones of the hoped-for deer herd, dead of its own too-much, bleach with the bones of the dead sage, or molder under the high-lined junipers.

I now suspect that just as a deer herd lives in mortal fear of its wolves, so does a mountain live in mortal fear of its deer. And perhaps with better cause, for while a buck pulled down by wolves can be replaced in two or three years, a range pulled down by too many deer may fail of replacement in as many decades.

So also with cows. The cowman who cleans his range of wolves does not realize that he is taking over the wolf's job of trimming the herd to fit the range. He has not learned to think like a mountain. Hence we have dustbowls, and rivers washing the future into the sea.

WE ALL STRIVE for safety, prosperity, comfort, long life, and dullness. The deer strives with his supple legs, the cowman with trap and poison, the statesman with pen, the most of us with machines, votes, and dollars, but it all comes to the same thing: peace in our time. A measure of success in this is all well enough, and perhaps is a requisite to objective thinking, but too much safety seems to yield only danger in the long run. Perhaps this is behind Thoreau's dictum: In wildness is the salvation of the world. Perhaps this is the hidden meaning in the howl of the wolf, long known among mountains, but seldom perceived among men.

AT CRYSTAL
MOUNTAIN

PETER MATTHIESSEN

Novelist, explorer, and naturalist Peter Matthiessen has also been a commercial fisherman and captain of a charter boat. He co-founded *The Paris Review* in 1953, the year before his first novel, *Race Rock*, was published. Other novels include *At Play in the Fields of the Lord* (1965), *Far Tortuga* (1975), and *Killing Mister Watson* (1990). His many nonfiction books have arisen from his travels of exploration. Among them are *Blue Meridian* (1971); *The Cloud Forest: A Chronicle of the South American Wilderness* (1961); and *The Snow Leopard* (1978), which includes this description of an exhausting trek through Nepal with conservationist George Schaller for a glimpse of the Himalayan blue sheep and the rare snow leopard.

•   •   •

NOVEMBER 1

This Black Pond Camp, though well below the Kang Pass, lies at an altitude of 17,000 feet, and an hour after the sun sinks behind the peaks, my wet boots have turned to blocks of ice.

GS's thermometer registers −20° Centigrade (4° below zero Fahrenheit) and though I wear everything I have, I quake with cold all night. Dawn comes at last, but making hot water from a pot of ice is difficult at this altitude, and it is past nine before boots are thawed and we are under way.

The snow bowl is the head of an ice river that descends a deep canyon to Shey. In the canyon we meet Jang-bu and Phu-Tsering, on their way up to fetch some food and pots: Dawa, they say, is down again with acute snow blindness.

Sherpa tracks in the frozen shadows follow the glassy boulders of the stream edge, and somewhere along the way I slip, losing the hoopoe feather that adorned my cap. The river falls steeply, for Shey lies three thousand feet below Kang La, and in the deep snow, the going is so treacherous that the sherpas have made no path; each man flounders through the drifts as best he can. Eventually, from a high corner of the canyon, rough red-brown lumps of human habitation come in view. The monastery stands like a small fort on a bluff where another river flows in from the east; a mile below, the rivers vanish into a deep and dark ravine. Excepting the lower slopes of the mountainside behind the monastery, which is open to the south, most of this treeless waste lies under snow, broken here and there by calligraphic patterns of bare rock, in an atmosphere so wild and desolate as to overwhelm the small huddle of dwellings.

High to the west, a white pyramid sails on the sky—the Crystal Mountain. In summer, this monument of rock is a shrine for pilgrims from all over Dolpo and beyond, who come here to make a prescribed circle around the Crystal Mountain and attend a holy festival at Shey. What is stirring about this peak, in snow time, is its powerful shape, which even today, with no clouds passing, makes it appear to be forging through the blue. "The power of such a mountain is so great and yet so subtle that, without compulsion, people are drawn to it from near and far, as if by the force of some invisible magnet; and they will undergo untold hardships and privations in their inexplicable urge to approach and to worship the centre of this sacred power... This worshipful or religious attitude is not impressed by scientific facts, like figures of altitude, which are foremost in the mind of modern man. Nor is it motivated by the urge to 'conquer' the mountain..."

A gravel island under Shey is reached by crossing ice and stones of a shallow channel. At the island's lower end are prayer walls and a stone stockade for animals; farther on, small conduits divert a flow of river water to a group of prayer mills in the form of waterwheels, each one housed separately in its own stone shrine. The conduits are frozen and the wheels are still. On top of the small stupas are offerings of white quartz crystals, presumably taken from the Crystal Mountain in the summer, when the five wheels spin five ancient prayer drums, sending OM MANI PADME HUM down the cold canyon.

On the far side of a plank bridge, a path climbs the bank to two big red-and-white entrance stupas on the bluff: I go up slowly. Prayer flags snap thinly on the wind, and a wind-bell has a wooden wing in the shape of a half-moon that moves the clapper; over the glacial rumble on the river stones, the wistful ring on the light wind is the first sound that is heard here at Shey Gompa.

The cluster of a half-dozen stone houses is stained red, in sign that Shey is a monastery, not a village. Another group of five small houses sits higher up the mountain; above this hamlet, a band of blue sheep may be seen with the naked eye. Across the river to the north, stuck on a cliff face at the portals of the canyon, is a red hermitage. Otherwise, except for prayer walls and the stone corrals, there are only the mighty rock formations and dry treeless mountainside where snow has melted, and the snow and sky.

I move on slowly, dull in mind and body. Gazing back up the Black River toward the rampart of icy cornices, I understand that we have come over the Kanjirobas to the mountain deserts of the Tibetan Plateau: we have crossed the Himalaya from south to north. But not until I had to climb this short steep path from the wintry river to the bluffs did I realize how tired I was after thirty-five days of hard trekking. And here I am, on this first day of November, standing before the Crystal Monastery, with its strange stones and flags and bells under the snows.

The monastery temple with its attached houses forms a sort of open court facing the south. Two women and two infants, sitting in the sun, make no sign of welcome. Fearing Kham-pa brigands, the women had locked themselves into their houses a few days ago, when Jang-bu and GS first appeared, and plainly they are still suspicious of our seemingly inexplicable mission. The younger woman is weaving a rough cloth on an ancient loom. When I say, "*Namaste!*" she repeats it, as if trying the word out. Three scraggy *dzos* and an old black nanny goat excepted, these are the only sentient beings left at Shey, which its inhabitants call Somdo, or "Confluence," because of the meeting of rivers beneath its bluff—the Kangju, "Snow Waters" (the one I think of as Black River, because of the black pond at its head, and the black eagle, and the black patterns of its stones and ice in the dark canyon), and the Yeju, "Low Waters" (which I shall call White River, because it comes down from the eastern snows).

NOVEMBER 2

. . . This morning I bathe inside my sunny tent and sort out gear. Dawa is still groaning with snow blindness, but Jang-bu and Phu-Tsering have crossed Black River to hunt scraps of low shrub juniper for firewood, and GS is up on this Somdo mountainside viewing his sheep; he returns half-frozen toward midmorning. After a quick meal of chapatis, we set off on a survey of other sheep populations in the region, heading eastward up the Saldang trail, which follows the north bank of the White River. Like the Saure and other east-west rivers in this season, this one is snowbound on the side that faces north, and across the water we can see snow tracks of marmot, wandering outward in weird patterns from a burrow; perhaps the animals, sent underground too early by those blizzards of the late monsoon, had gone out foraging. But they are hibernated now, there is no fresh marmot sign, the land seems empty.

Snow clouds come up over the mountains, and the shining river turns to black, over black rocks. A lone black *dzo* nuzzles the stony earth. GS has picked up scat of a large carnivore and turns it in his hand, wondering aloud why fox sign, so abundant at Black Pond, is uncommon here at lower altitudes. "Too big for fox, I think..."

As GS speaks, I scan the mountain slopes for bharal: on these rolling hills to the east of Somdo, we have not seen even one. Abruptly, he says, "Hold it! Freeze! Two snow leopard!" I see a pale shape slip behind a low rise patched with snow, as GS, agitated, mutters, "Tail's too short! Must have been foxes—!"

"No!" I say. "Much too big—!"

"Wolves!" he cries out. "Wolves!"

And there they are.

Moving away without haste up an open slope beyond the rise, the wolves bring the barren hills to life. Two on the slope to northward frisk and play, but soon they pause to look us over; their tameness is astonishing. Then they cut across the hill to join three others that are climbing a stone gully. The pack stops each little while to gaze at us, and through the telescope we rejoice in every shining hair: two silver wolves, and two of faded gold, and one that is the no-color of frost; this frost-colored wolf, a big male, seems to be leader. All have black tail tips and a delicate black fretting on the back. "That's why there's no sign of fox or leopard!" GS says, "and that's why the blue sheep stay near the river cliffs, away from this open country!" I ask if the wolves would hunt and kill the fox and leopard, and he says they would. For some reason, the wolves' appearance here has taken us by surprise; it is in Tibet that such mythic creatures belong. This is an Asian race of *Canis lupus*, the timber wolf, which both of us have seen in Alaska, and it is always an exciting animal: the empty hills where the pack has gone have come to life. In a snow patch are five sets of wolf tracks, and old wolf scats along the path contain brittle gray stuff and soft yellow hair—blue sheep and marmot.

NOVEMBER 3

There is so much that enchants me in this spare, silent place that I move softly so as not to break a spell. Because the taking of life has been forbidden by the Lama of Shey, bharal and wolves alike draw near the monastery. On the hills and in the stone beds of the river are fossils from blue ancient days when all this soaring rock lay beneath the sea. And all about are the prayer stones, prayer flags, prayer wheels, and prayer mills in the torrent, calling on all the elements in nature to join in celebration of the One. What I hear from my tent is a delicate wind-bell and the river from the east, in this easterly wind that may bring a change in the weather. At daybreak, two great ravens come, their long toes scratching on the prayer walls.

The sun refracts from the white glaze of the mountains, chills the air. Old Sonam, who lives alone in the hamlet up the hill, was on the mountain before day, gathering the summer's dung to dry and store as cooking fuel; what I took for lumpish matter straightens on the sky as the sun rises, setting her gaunt silhouette afire.

Eleven sheep are visible on the Somdo slope above the monastery, six rams together and a group of ewes and young; though the bands begin to draw near to one another and sniff urine traces, there is no real sign of rut. From our lookout above Sonam's house, three more groups—six, fourteen, and twenty-six—can be seen on the westward slopes, across Black River.

Unable to hold the scope on the restless animals, GS calls out to me to shift the binoculars from the band of fourteen to the group of six sheep directly across the river from our lookout. "Why are those sheep running?" he demands and a moment later hollers, "Wolves!" All six sheep are springing for the cliffs, but a pair of wolves coming straight downhill are cutting off the rearmost animal as it bounds across a stretch of snow toward the ledges. In the hard light, the blue-gray creature seems far too swift to catch, yet the streaming wolves gain ground on the hard snow. Then they are whisking through the matted juniper and down over steepening rocks, and it appears that the bharal will be cut off and bowled over, down the mountain, but at the last moment it scoots free and gains a narrow ledge where no wolf can follow.

In the frozen air, the whole mountain is taut; the silence rings. The sheep's flanks quake, and the wolves are panting; otherwise, all is still, as if the arrangement of pale shapes held the world together. Then I breathe, and the mountain breathes, setting the world in motion once again.

Briefly, the wolves gaze about, then make their way up the mountainside in the unhurried gait that may carry them fifty miles in a single day. Two pack mates join them, and in high yak pasture the four pause to romp and roll in dung. Two of these were not among the five seen yesterday, and we recall that the old woman had seen seven. Then they trot onward, disappearing behind a ridge of snow. The band of fourteen sheep high on this ridge gives a brief run of alarm, then forms a line on a high point to stare down at the wolves and watch them go. Before long, all are browsing once again, including the six that were chased onto the precipice.

Turning to speak, we just shake our heads and grin. "It was worth walking five weeks just to see that," GS sighs at last. "That was the most exciting wolf hunt I ever saw." And a little later, exhilarated still, he wonders aloud if I remember "that rainy afternoon in the Serengeti when we watched wild dogs make a zebra kill in that strange storm light on the plain, and all those thousands of animals running?" I nod. I am still excited by the wolves seen so close yesterday, and to see them again, to watch them hunt blue sheep in such fashion, flying down across the cliffs within sight of our tents at Shey Gompa—what happiness!

NOVEMBER 6

The nights at Shey are rigid, under rigid stars; the fall of a wolf pad on the frozen path might be heard up and down the canyon. But a hard wind comes before the dawn to rattle the tent canvas, and this morning it is clear again, and colder. At daybreak, the White River, just below, is sheathed in ice, with scarcely a murmur from the stream beneath.

The two ravens come to tritons on the gompa roof. *Gorawk, gorawk,* they croak, and this is the name given to them by the sherpas. Amidst the prayer flags and great horns of Tibetan argali, the gorawks greet first light with an odd musical double-note—*a-ho*—that emerges as if by miracle from those ragged throats. Before sunrise every day, the great blackbirds are gone, like the last tatters of departing night.

The sun rising at the head of the White River brings a suffused glow to the tent canvas, and the robin accentor flits away across the frozen yard. At seven, there is breakfast in the cook hut—tea and porridge—and after breakfast on most days I watch sheep with GS, parting company with him after a while, when the sheep lie down, to go off on some expedition of my own. Often I scan the caves and ledges on the far side of Black River in the hope of leopard; I am alert for fossils, wolves, and birds. Sometimes I observe the sky and mountains, and sometimes I sit in meditation, doing my best to empty out my mind, to attain that state in which everything is "at rest, free, and immortal... All things abided eternally as they were in their proper places... something infinite behind everything appeared." (No Buddhist said this, but a seventeenth-century Briton.) And soon all sounds, and all one sees and feels, take on imminence, and immanence, as if the Universe were coming to attention, a Universe of which one is the center, a Universe that is not the same and yet not different from oneself, even from a scientific point of view: within man as within mountains there are many parts of hydrogen and oxygen, of calcium, phosphorus, potassium, and other elements. "You never enjoy the world aright, till the Sea itself flows in your veins, till you are clothed with the heavens, and crowned with the stars: and perceive yourself to be the sole heir of the whole world, and more than so, because men are in it who are every one sole heirs as well as you."

I have a meditation place on Somdo mountain, a broken rock outcrop like an altar set into the hillside, protected from all but the south wind by shards of granite and dense thorn. In the full sun it is warm, and its rock crannies give shelter to small stunted plants that cling to this desert mountainside—dead red-brown stalks of a wild buckwheat (*Polygonum*), some shrubby cinquefoil, pale edelweiss, and everlasting, and even a few poor wisps of *Cannabis*. I arrange a rude rock seat as a lookout on the world, set out binoculars in case wild creatures should happen into view, then cross my legs and regulate my breath, until I scarcely breathe at all.

Now the mountains all around me take on life; the Crystal Mountain moves. Soon there comes the murmur of the torrent, from far away below under the ice: it seems impossible that I can hear this sound. Even in windlessness, the sound of rivers comes and goes and falls and rises, like the wind itself. An instinct comes to open outward by letting all life in, just as a flower fills with sun. To burst forth from this old husk and cast one's energy abroad, to fly. . .

Although I am not conscious of emotion, the mind-opening brings a soft mist to my eyes. Then the mist passes, the cold wind clears my head, and body-mind comes and goes on the light air. A sun-filled Buddha. One day I shall meditate in falling snow.

I lower my gaze from the snow peaks to the glistening thorns, the snow patches, the lichens. Though I am blind to it, the Truth is near, in the reality of what I sit on—rocks. These hard rocks instruct my bones in what my brain could never grasp in the Heart Sutra that "form is emptiness, and emptiness is form"— the Void, the emptiness of blue-black space, contained in everything. Sometimes when I meditate, the big rocks dance.

The secret of the mountains is that the mountains simply exist, as I do myself: the mountains exist simply, which I do not. The mountains have no "meaning," they *are* meaning; the mountains *are*. The sun is round. I ring with life, and the mountains ring, and when I can hear it, there is a ringing that we share. I understand all this not in my mind but in my heart, knowing how meaningless it is to try to capture what cannot be expressed, knowing that mere words will remain when I read it all again, another day.

KILIMANJARO

MICHAEL CRICHTON

B orn in Chicago in 1942, Crichton was visiting lecturer in anthropology
at Cambridge and a graduate of Harvard Medical School before writing such works of "techno-fiction" as *The Andromeda Strain* (1969), *Congo*
(1980), and *Jurassic Park* (1990). He is also the creator of the popular television series *ER*, and probably the only novelist to have a dinosaur named
after him, the ankylosaur *Crichtonsaurus bohini*, discovered in 2002. His
nonfiction works include *Five Patients: The Hospital Explained* (1970); *Jas-
per Jones* (1977); and *Travels* (1988), a lively account of his various real-life
adventures—including this one, which describes what he thought would be
an easy amble up Tanzania's deceptive Mount Kilimanjaro, which at 19,335
feet is Africa's highest peak.

. . .

THE GROUP STARTS from the hotel at a brisk pace. Little
children from nearby villages walk with us, chatter in broken
English, beg. The sun is shining; the warm morning carries an

air of expectation, of adventure. I am terrifically excited. I have never done anything like this in my life and I am sure it will be rewarding.

In less than an hour my enthusiasm is gone. The begging children have become reminders that we are not trailblazers, but more like commuters en route to a well-established tourist destination. I find their cuteness irritating, because it has been honed on my predecessors and thus reminds me that thousands have gone before me.

The atmospheric haze has closed in; we can no longer see the mountain that is our destination. We are walking up a dusty road through poor farming villages, the views are not attractive, and the day has turned from warm to hot. I am sweating profusely. My clothing chafes at waist and crotch and armpits. What's worse, I feel blisters on my feet, though I have not been walking for an hour.

I stop by the side of the road, pull off my boots, and inspect my feet. Loren tells me I should have worn two pairs of socks, a thin inner one and a heavy outer one; I dismiss this double-sock camping lore with a wave. My feet will be all right; I'll put Band-Aids on them in the evening. Paul walks by, mentions he has some moleskin if I need it; I say no thanks, wondering to myself what moleskin is. I have never heard of moleskin.

I keep walking.

We enter the rain forest on the lower slopes of Kilimanjaro. It is a beautiful and lush setting, gurgling streams and hanging moss on huge trees that arch overhead and block the sun. It is cooler here, and the trail follows a fresh stream. Monkeys chatter in the trees. I feel renewed enthusiasm. However, before long the humidity, the moisture trapped beneath the canopy of the trees, the dripping of water like a constant rain, gets on my nerves. My clothes are now entirely soaked. I no longer appreciate the beauty, no longer enjoy the clear water tumbling over the smooth rocks. And my feet hurt more and more.

It was a relief to enter the rain forest, and it is a relief to leave it in early afternoon, emerging into an open meadow of grass six feet high. However, by now I am very tired—astonishingly tired—and the path up the meadow is steep. I am wondering how much farther I must go. There are no signposts to tell me how I am doing, how far before we reach the huts. Unable to plan, unable to pace myself, I find my fatigue feels extreme. Do I have an hour still to go? Two hours? Then I see, on a ridge above the high grass, the brown geometric A-frames of the Mandara huts. They are very close. It is only four o'clock in the afternoon. I am not really so tired after all.

We have afternoon tea. Paul and Jan have been here for an hour, so much faster was their pace. The Mandara huts are at nine thousand feet, so I have a chance to feel the altitude. It doesn't seem to make much difference. My spirits are good as I walk around the huts, looking around.

The only problem is my feet. They hurt considerably, and when I remove my boots I find that I have large blisters on the heels and on the small toes of both feet. I put Band-Aids on them, eat an early dinner of bread and canned beef stew, and go to sleep. Paul says he never sleeps well at altitude. I sleep badly.

I'm nervous about the coming day.

THE SECOND DAY is strikingly different. On the first day, the landscape was varied—from desert savanna to rain forest to mountain meadow—but there was never any wider view, never any orientation, any sense of where you were on the mountain. You were just climbing.

On the second day, the landscape is unchanging alpine meadows. An hour from the huts, we suddenly see the peak of Kilimanjaro with perfect clarity, the sides of the volcano streaked with snow. I am excited. We stop for pictures. Here, in a field of low grass, with open topography, I can see where I am—moving on the flank of an enormous wide cone. But so wide is this volcano, and so gentle its slopes, that soon we cannot see the peak any more; it is somewhere ahead, hidden behind deceptively gentle ridges. Once again, deprived of a view of my destination, I am discouraged, and ask the guides when we will be able to see Kilimanjaro.

They invariably point to the ground beneath my feet and say, "*This* Kilimanjaro." When I make myself clear, they shrug. They don't seem to understand my anxiety about seeing the mountain when I am walking on it. Finally our guide, Julius, says, "You see the top with snow tomorrow, all day tomorrow. Not today, but from tomorrow."

I walk on. It is never really hot today, and the walking is pleasant, the ground dark and spongy underfoot. Occasionally the trail is a knee-deep trench dug by all the feet that have passed before. And we are seeing more people on the trails, too:

apparently climbers from other hotels. All sorts of people, all sorts of ages. I am encouraged by the diversity.

All in all it is a pleasant day. My only concern is my feet, which are painful. Today I am wearing sneakers instead of boots, but the damage is already done. And I am often winded; I stop to rest every fifteen or twenty minutes. Loren never seems to tire, but I am thirty-three, she is twenty-two. Even so, as the day goes on, I notice she appreciates my frequent stops.

In the absence of the peak, I am looking for the lobelia trees, which I have been told characteristically appear at the eleven-thousand-foot level. I don't know what lobelia trees look like, and since we are above the tree line, every kind of odd plant receives my scrutiny. I ask the guides, "Lobelia? Lobelia?" and they just shake their heads.

Finally, when we break for a late lunch, we find ourselves sitting next to a light-green plant about four feet high with puffy, bulbous leaves. Julius points it out as lobelia.

At every break, the guides and porters sit and smoke cigarettes. I can't believe they are doing this. I am gasping and wheezing and stopping for breath every fifteen minutes. The lobelias at eleven thousand feet mean, I remind myself, that I am barely halfway up.

I begin to wonder if I can make it to the top, after all.

During the rest of the day, I have nothing left to look for except the Horomba huts where we will stay the night. When we reach them, I am extremely tired, and my feet are very painful.

The location of the huts is spectacular, A-frames set on a ledge of black lava at 12,300 feet, looking down on a bank of clouds. At sunset, the air is pink and purple. I feel I am walking around at an altitude normally reached only by airplanes; it is exhilarating. It's also making me light-headed. Now that I am just strolling around the camp and not pushing along the trail, I realize how severely the altitude affects me. I can't breathe comfortably, even sitting down. A term comes back from medical school: "resting dyspnea," shortness of breath while sitting down. I never appreciated how panicky it feels not to be able to catch your breath.

I wonder about altitude sickness, which starts to be a problem at this height. Altitude sickness makes your lungs fill up with water. The cause is unknown, but if you have a dry cough or a headache, you must head back down at once or you may die. I give an experimental cough. I don't have altitude sickness.

My feet are my real concern. I am reluctant to take my sneakers off and see the extent of the damage. When I finally do, I find that the Band-Aids have shifted and done little to protect me; the blisters are larger than yesterday and they have burst, exposing red, inflamed, exquisitely tender skin.

It's sufficiently bad that I abandon my pride and ask Paul for help. He takes one look and calls Jan, who is, after all, a surgeon. Jan gets out his moleskin—moleskin turns out to be a thin, padded cotton sheet with adhesive on one side—and cuts pieces to fit my blisters. We use all his moleskin fixing me up. He stands back and pronounces himself satisfied with the dressing.

I thank him.

"Yes," he says sadly, "but it is too bad."

"Why?"

"Well," he says, looking at my feet, "now you must go back."

"No," I say.

"I think," he says judiciously, "that you cannot go on with your feet this way. You must go down the mountain tomorrow."

"No," I say. "I'll continue." I am surprised at the strength of my own conviction, sitting there with my feet bandaged and my breathing labored. But it doesn't really feel like conviction, it just feels like logic. I've already walked two days. If I go back, it will take two days. That's four days. Whereas, if I push on an extra day, in a total of five days I will have reached the summit and returned.

I've gone too far to turn back, at least in my own mind.

Jan leaves. Pretty soon Loren comes over. "I talked to Jan. He's very worried about your feet."

"Uh-huh."

"Jan says you could get a bad infection. He says the dirt from the trail gets ground into your open skin and you could get a serious infection."

I wonder where she is leading with this.

"I've already talked to the guide," she says, "and it's no problem. They do it all the time. They'll send one porter back down with you, so you don't need to worry about getting lost. And don't worry about me; Paul and Jan will keep an eye on me, and I'll be fine."

Her whole attitude is so casual. Climbing this mountain just doesn't mean that much to her. I wonder why it means so much to me.

"I'm not going back," I say. Even as I say it, I realize I am being unrealistic. We are at 12,300 feet on the side of a mountain. I have very bad blisters. She's right: I should go back.

"Your feet look so awful. Are you sure?"

"I'm sure."

"Okay," she says. "I guess you know what you're doing."

"I do."

"They say tomorrow is the worst day," she says.

"That's fine," I say. "I'll be ready."

WE START EARLY on the third day. The terrain turns abruptly vertical; for an hour we scramble hand over foot up lava ledges. The air becomes much colder; we start out in sweaters but soon we are wearing parkas; then gloves, then hoods.

After two hours, we break out of the narrow lava ledges onto the saddle. It is an abrupt and startling view; at last I can see the geography.

Mount Kilimanjaro is actually two major peaks. Kibo is a broad cinder cone with snow on its southern flanks. A few miles to the east, an older volcanic peak, Mawenzi, presents a different appearance—jagged, harsh vertical lines and streaks of snow over crumbling, rocky pinnacles. Mawenzi is about 16,900 feet high, and Kibo 19,340. The two peaks are separated by a distance of seven miles, and between them lies a sloping desert plateau averaging about thirteen thousand feet in altitude, called the "saddle."

It is here that we have emerged, at the base of Mawenzi, looking across the windswept saddle toward Kibo, its blunt summit cloudless in early morning. The view is spectacular in a bleak way. For the first time on the trip, I appreciate my vulnerability in a hostile environment. I am standing on a desert plateau two and a half miles high. There are no trees, no plants, no life at all, just red rocks and sand and freezing wind. Ahead of me, at the base of Kibo, I see a sparkling dot—the tin roof of tiny Kibo Hut, where we will spend the night before making the ascent in darkness up the cinder cone the following day.

The clothing that was once too hot, that clung and chafed, is now flimsy as paper before the wind. I am chilled; I put on everything I am carrying in my day pack, and Loren and I set out across the saddle.

Even walking on flat terrain is difficult at this altitude, and Loren calls for a rest—the first time on the trip she has done so. After midday, clouds appear around the peaks, and cast swift-moving shadows on the desert floor. We are now on a gentle rise up to the hut at 15,500 feet. Distances are deceptive here; the hut looks only an hour distant, but after an hour it still seems no closer.

We walk slower and slower, and when we finally come up to Kibo Hut to greet Paul and Jan, who have been here for a while, we feel as if we are moving in slow motion. Paradoxically, the thin air makes us behave as if we were underwater, in a dense medium.

Paul and Jan have lost their usual good spirits. In fact, everyone is distinctly irritable as they trudge up to the hut. People complain—about the wind, the bunks, the food, the weather. The general mood is grim. Paul says, "I've seen it before. It's the altitude. Makes you irritable. And, of course, everyone's wondering."

"Wondering?"

"Whether they'll make it to the top."

That's certainly what I am wondering, but Paul is an experienced climber who's been on several trekking expeditions in Nepal. "*You're* worried about it?"

"Not really. But it crosses your mind. It has to."

The accommodations at Kibo Hut are reminiscent of a Siberian prison camp. Triple-decker bunks line all four tin walls; in the middle of the room, a central pit for eating. The wind whines through the cracks in the walls; nobody removes any clothing indoors. We have dinner at 5:00 PM, porridge and tea. Nobody can eat much. We are all thinking about the ascent. We must reach the top before ten the next morning, because after that the weather is likely to sock in, closing off the views and making the summit dangerous. If we climb too slowly, we risk being turned back from the summit because of the weather.

One of the guides tells us the plan: we will be awakened with tea (no coffee at these altitudes) at 2:00 PM, and we will begin our ascent in darkness. One lantern for every two people. We will stay together, so as not to get lost in the darkness. It is six hours from here to the summit; after three hours, there is a cave where we can stop and rest, but otherwise there is no shelter until we reach the summit, and come back down to Kibo. It will be very cold. We should wear all the clothing we have.

I'm already wearing all the clothing I have. I'm wearing long johns and three pairs of pants, two tee shirts, two shirts, a sweater, and a parka. I wear a wool balaclava on my head. I wear all these clothes to bed, removing only my boots before climbing into my sleeping bag. Everyone else wears their clothes to bed, too. We're in bed by 7:00 PM, silent, listening to the wind whine.

Sleep is impossible. Every time I begin to drift off, I snap awake, suddenly fearful, convinced I am suffocating, only to realize that it is simply the altitude.

I am not the only one with this problem. Inside the darkened hut, I hear groans and curses in a half-dozen languages throughout the night. It is almost a relief when the guide shakes me, hands me a plastic cup filled with smoky hot tea, and tells me to dress.

All around me, people are pulling on boots and gloves. Nobody speaks. The atmosphere is, if anything, even more grim than before. Paul stops by to wish us good luck on our ascent; he hopes we make it. I wonder if it's some sort of mountaineering tradition, this last-minutes wishing of luck. After all, we've come so far, there is so little left, who would turn back now? Nobody in his right mind. After all, I think, how bad can it be?

We take our lanterns and leave the tin hut, and climb the mountain in darkness.

VERY QUICKLY it becomes a nightmare. The lantern is useless; the wind blows it out; the darkness is total. I cannot see anything and continually stumble over rocks and small obstacles. I am sure this would be painful if I could feel anything in my feet at all, but they are numb with cold. Even when I wiggle my toes in the boots, I feel nothing. As I stumble up the mountain, the numb cold creeps up my legs, first to the shins, then the knees, then the mid-thigh. The trail upward is steep and exhausting, but the cold is so penetrating we stop for only a few moments at a time, just enough to catch our breath in the blackness, and stumble on. I feel rather than see the presence of the guides, the porters, the other hikers. Occasionally I hear a grunt or a voice, but for the most part everyone trudges along silently; I hear only the wind and my own laboured breathing. As I walk along, I have plenty of time to wonder whether I am getting frostbite in my numb feet. It's my own fault—I was completely unprepared for this trip, I didn't bring the right equipment, including the right boots; it was a serious oversight; I may be penalized now. Anyway, frostbite or not, I am having real trouble. I frankly don't think I'll be able to make it. I can go on for a while, but I doubt I can last much longer.

Somewhere around me, I hear Loren. "Is that you?"

"Yes," I say. "Can you feel your feet?"

"I haven't been able to feel them for an hour," she says. There is a pause. "*Listen, what are we doing here?*"

The question takes me by surprise. I don't really have an answer. "We're having an adventure," I say, and laugh cheerfully.

She doesn't laugh back.

"This is crazy," she says. "Climbing this mountain is crazy."

Her words enter my consciousness directly. I have no doubt in my mind she is right. It is crazy to be doing this. Yet I feel protective toward the decision to make the climb, as if it were a friend I don't want criticized.

I am trudging onward in the darkness, tired, numb, gasping for air, freezing cold, a prisoner on a forced march. I put one foot in front of the other. One foot in front of the other. I try to set a rhythm, to keep moving forward in that rhythm.

To consider whether or not this is crazy does not help my rhythm right now. I ignore her statement and concentrate on walking in my rhythm. How long I continue in this way I am not sure; it is too much trouble to look at my watch: clumsily peeling away layers of clothing to expose a glowing green dial that is hard to read through chilled, tearing eyes. After a while the time doesn't matter any more; I just keep walking.

The arrival at the cave at the halfway point is a surprise. The cave isn't warm, but it's out of the wind and so seems warmer. We are all able to light our lanterns, so we have light. We can look at one another. People huddle together, talking quietly. I see the shock on many faces. I am not the only one who finds this climb a nightmare.

Loren sits next to me, whispers, "I hear the English couple is going back."

"Oh?"

"She's sick. She's throwing up from the altitude."

"Oh." I don't know who she is talking about. I don't really care.

"How do you feel?" she says.

"Terrible."

"How're your feet?"

"Blocks of ice."

A pause, and then she says, "Listen, let's go back."

I am shocked. This woman who has so much energy, is so much in control of her body, now wants to quit. She's had it. She wants to quit.

"Listen," she says, "I'm not embarrassed to say we got to seventeen thousand feet and then quit. We're not in shape. Seventeen thousand is damned good."

I don't know what to say. She's right. I think it over.

Loren continues quickly, "It's insane to be doing this. There's no reason to be doing this. It's some kind of crazy proving of ourselves—for what? Who cares? Really. Let's go back. We'll tell everyone we climbed it. Who will know? It won't matter. Nobody will ever know."

All I can think is: *I'll know.*

And I think of a lot of other things, about not being a quitter, and how I think that quitting is contagious, that once you start to quit it spreads through your life—but that's sports talk, coaching talk, I'm not sure I believe it.

What I believe is, *I'll know.* I feel trapped by an inner honesty I didn't know I had.

"I want to keep going," I say.

"Why?" she says. "Why is it so important to you to get to the top of some stupid mountain?"

"I'm here now, I might as well do it," I say. It sounds evasive. The fact is, I have no better answer. I have put up with a lot of pain and a lot of anxiety to get this far, and now I am in a cave in predawn darkness within a few hours of the summit, and there is no way I am going to quit now.

"Michael, this is crazy," she says.

The others are filing out of the cave, resuming their ascent. I get to my feet.

"Just go one more hour," I say. "You can make it another hour. Then, if you still want to go back, we will." I figure in another hour it will be dawn, and everything will seem better to her, and she will be encouraged to go on. I figure she'll never quit if she knows that I am continuing.

And I am continuing. I surprise myself with my own strength and conviction.

DAWN IS A beautiful prismatic band that throws the jagged peak of Mawenzi into relief. I tell myself I should pause for a moment to enjoy it. I can't. I tell myself I should pause and take a picture of it, so I can enjoy the picture later. I can't even take a picture. I have lost the ability to do anything that some animal part of my brain judges to be nonessential energetic movement. It is not necessary to take a picture. I don't take one.

A few thoughts enter my awareness anyway. I have never seen a sky so indigo-black. It looks like the sky from space pictures—and I realize that it should, that I am now more than three miles above the surface of the earth, and the normal blue sky, created by atmosphere and suspended dust, is gone.

The other thing is that the horizon is curved. There is no doubt about it. Sunrise is an arc that bends down at the sides. I can see with my own eyes that I am standing on a spherical planet. But the actual sensation is uncomfortable, as if I am viewing the world through one of those curving wide-angle lenses. I look away.

I put one foot in front of the other, one foot in front of the other. I lean on my walking stick and breathe and keep my rhythm. I wait for the air to warm; eventually it does, a little. At least I can see where I am walking. But when I look up, the summit seems far away. Most of the other climbers are farther along, and their bright jackets contrast with the beige scree of the volcano.

"Scree" is a geological term for small cinders of volcanic origin. We are walking up, ankle-deep in scree. It is like walking on a vertical beach. You take two steps up, and slide one step back. Two steps up, one back. The destination never comes any nearer.

Two hours after sunrise is the worst time for me. I am utterly exhausted, and I am suddenly aware, looking at the climbers farther up the slopes, that they are walking like mountaineers in a *National Geographic* special. One of those movies where the intrepid climbers plod through the snow, head down, with a dogged, deliberate rhythm. Step, breathe, breathe. Step, breathe, breathe.

The hikers above me are moving like that. And so am I. I have become a character in a television special. I am totally out of my element. Loren is right—I never expected it would be this hard. I'm not cut out for this. I'm not in shape for this. I'm not interested in doing this, now or ever again. Who cares about this climbing business anyway? A million people have already climbed Kilimanjaro, there's nothing special to it. There's no real accomplishment. It's no big deal.

My guide, Julius, sees that I am fatigued. He offered to push me. I tell him no. He offers to push Loren, and she agrees, and he stands behind her with his arms on her waist and pushes her up the slope. But it doesn't seem to me that he helps Loren. It seems to me that you have to do this one alone.

Pretty soon Loren tells Julius to stop pushing her, and she continues by herself. She doesn't seem to be aware of me any more, although we are only a few feet apart. She is lost in some private world of focused effort.

I am trying to figure out what is going on inside my head. I have begun to understand that climbing at altitude is a mental process, an exercise in concentration and will. I notice that some thoughts sap my energy, but others allow me to continue for five or ten minutes without stopping. I am trying to figure out which thoughts work best.

To my surprise, the mental pep talks ("You can do it, you're doing great, keep up the good work") don't help. They just provoke the counter-thought that I am kidding myself and will ultimately fail.

Nor does focusing on my rhythm, my pace, counting my steps or my breathing, going for a kind of mindlessness. That just puts everything into mental neutrality, which is not bad, but not particularly good, either.

Equally surprising, to focus on my exhaustion is not dele-terious. I can think, God, my legs ache, I don't think I can lift them another step, and it doesn't slow me down. It's the truth, and my legs don't feel worse just because I think the truth.

In the end, what seems to work is to think of a nice warm swimming pool in California. Or the nice beer and curry din-ner I will have when I get back to civilization. Hawaiian palm trees and surf. Scuba diving. Something far from my present surroundings. A pleasant fantasy or daydream.

So I think about swimming pools and palm trees as I plod up the gritty scree. Around 8:00 AM, Julius begins to show concern. Already people are coming down from the summit—I resent them deeply—and Julius wants to make sure we reach the top before any bad weather closes in. I ask him how far away the summit is. He says forty-five minutes.

He has been saying forty-five minutes for the last two hours.

In a way, it's not his fault. The higher slopes of Kilimanjaro provide a bizarrely undramatic perspective. It's like the view an ant would have on the outside of an overturned salad bowl—all you see is a curved surface that gets narrower as you approach the top, but otherwise looks pretty much the same all the time.

It's very dramatic to *be* there, because your body can feel the steepness of the ascent, and it is dizzying to look up to the climbers above you. But it doesn't *look* like much at all.

Julius begins to urge us onward, bribing us with chocolate bars, threatening us with clouds. He needn't bother. We are going as fast as we possibly can, and finally, around 9:00 AM, we arrive at Gillman's Point, marked by a small concrete plaque at 18,700 feet. Although the actual summit, Uhuru Point, is at 19,340 feet, most hikers stop at Gillman's Point and consider honor satisfied. I certainly do.

I stand on the summit, pose for pictures, read the plaque, and look at the flags and mementos left by previous climbing groups. I stare indifferently at the views. I'm not elated, I'm not self-satisfied, I'm not anything. I'm just here at the summit. I have gotten here after all, and now I'm here.

Loren tells me I have gotten her to the top, and I tell her she did it herself. We take pictures of each other. And all the while I keep thinking one thing: I am here. I got here.

I am at the summit of Kilimanjaro.

EIGER DREAMS

JON KRAKAUER

Seattle-based Jon Krakauer is best known for *Into Thin Air,* his widely read account of the 1996 climbing tragedy on Mount Everest. Himself a respected mountaineer and a mountain writer—he has been awarded the American Alpine Club's Literary Award and contributes regularly to *Outside* and *Smithsonian* magazines—he has climbed and written about most of the world's highest peaks, including Denali, K2, which he describes as "a steep pyramid of brown rock and shining ice that straddles the Sino-Pakistani border," and, of course, 29,029-foot Everest. But the piece included here, from his 1990 book, *Eiger Dreams,* recounts his efforts to scale Switzerland's Mount Eiger, and is a reminder that not all mountain-climbing stories end in conquest and glory.

. . .

IN THE EARLY MOMENTS of *The Eiger Sanction,* Clint Eastwood saunters into the dimly lit headquarters of C-2 to find out who he is supposed to assassinate next. Dragon, the evil albino who runs the CIA-like organization, tells Eastwood that although the agency does not yet have the target's name, they have discovered that "our man will be involved in a climb in the Alps this summer. And we know which mountain he will climb: the Eiger."

Eastwood has no trouble guessing which route—"The North Face, of course"—and allows that he is familiar with that particular alpine wall: "I tried to climb it twice, it tried to kill me twice. . . Look, if the target's trying to climb the Eiger, chances are my work will be done for me."

The problem with climbing the North Face of the Eiger is that in addition to getting up 6,000 vertical feet of crumbling limestone and black ice, one must climb over some formidable mythology. The trickiest moves on any climb are the mental ones, the psychological gymnastics that keep terror in check, and the Eiger's grim aura is intimidating enough to rattle anyone's poise. The epics that have taken place on the Nordwand have been welded into the world's collective unconscious in grisly detail by more than two thousand newspaper and magazine articles. The dust jackets of books with titles such as *Eiger: Wall of Death*, remind us that the Nordwand "has defeated hundreds and killed forty-four. . .Those who fell were found— sometimes years later—desiccated and dismembered. The body of one Italian mountaineer hung from its rope, unreachable but visible to the curious below, for three years, alternately sealed into the ice sheath of the wall and swaying in the winds of summer."

The history of the mountain resonates with the struggles of such larger-than-life figures as Buhl, Bonatti, Messner, Rebuffat, Terray, Haston, and Harlin, not to mention Eastwood. The names of the landmarks on the face—the Hinterstoisser Traverse, the Ice Hose, the Death Bivouac, the White Spider— are household words among both active and armchair alpinists from Tokyo to Buenos Aires; the very mention of these places is enough to make any climber's hands turn clammy. The rockfall and avalanches that rain continuously down the Nordwand are legendary. So is the heavy weather: Even when the skies over the rest of Europe are cloudless, violent storms brew over the Eiger, like those dark clouds that hover eternally above Transylvanian castles in vampire movies.

Needless to say, all this makes the Eiger North Face one of the most widely coveted climbs in the world.

The Nordwand was first climbed in 1938, and since then it has had more than 150 ascents, among them a solo climb in 1983 that took all of five and a half hours, but don't try to tell Staff Sergeant Carlos J. Ragone, U.S.A.F., that the Eiger has become a scenic cruise. Last fall, Marc Twight and I were sitting outside our tents above Kleine Scheidegg, the cluster of hotels and restaurants at the foot of the Eiger, when Ragone strolled into camp under a bulging pack and announced that he had come to climb the Nordwand. In the discussion that ensued, we learned that he was AWOL from an air base in England. His commanding officer had refused to grant Ragone a leave when the CO learned what Ragone intended to do with it, but Ragone had left anyway. "Trying this climb will probably cost me my stripes," he said, "but on the other hand, if I get up the mother they might promote me."

Unfortunately, Ragone didn't get up the mother. September had gone down in the Swiss record books as the wettest since 1864, and the face was in atrocious condition, worse even than usual, plastered with rime and loaded with unstable snow. The weather forecast was for continuing snow and high wind. Two partners who were supposed to rendezvous with Ragone backed out because of the nasty conditions. Ragone, however, was not about to be deterred by the mere lack of company. On October 3 he started up the climb by himself. On the lower reaches of the face, near the top of a buttress known as the First Pillar, he made a misstep. His ice axes and crampons sheared out of the rotten ice, and Ragone found himself airborne. Five hundred vertical feet later he hit the ground.

Incredibly, his landing was cushioned by the accumulation of powder snow at the base of the wall, and Ragone was able to walk away from the fall with no more damage than bruises and a crimp in his back. He hobbled out of the blizzard into the *Bahnhof buffet,* asked for a room, went upstairs, and fell asleep. At some point during his tumble to the bottom of the wall he had lost an ice axe and his wallet, which contained all his identification and money. In the morning, when it was time to settle his room bill, all Ragone could offer for payment was his remaining ice axe. The *Bahnhof* manager was not amused. Before slinking out of Scheidegg, Ragone stopped by our camp to ask if we were interested in buying what was left of his climbing gear. We told him that we'd like to help him out, but we happened to be a little strapped for cash ourselves. In that case, Ragone, seeing as he didn't think he was going to feel like climbing again for a while, said he'd just give the stuff to us. "That mountain is a bastard," he spat, glancing up at the Nordwand one last time. With that, he limped off through the snow toward England to face the wrath of his CO.

LIKE RAGONE, Marc and I had come to Switzerland to climb the Nordwand. Marc, eight years my junior, sports two earrings in his left ear and a purple haircut that would do a punk rocker proud. He is also a red-hot climber. One of the differences between us was that Marc wanted very badly to climb the Eiger, while I wanted very badly only to have climbed the Eiger. Marc, understand, is at that age when the pituitary secretes an over-abundance of those hormones that mask the subtler emotions, such as fear. He tends to confuse things like life-or-death climbing with fun. As a friendly gesture, I planned to let Marc lead all the most fun pitches on the Nordwand.

Unlike Ragone, Marc and I were not willing to go up on the wall until conditions improved. Due to the Nordwand's concave architecture, whenever it snows, few places on the wall are not exposed to avalanches. In summer, if things go well, it will typically take a strong party two days, maybe three, to climb the Nordwand. In the fall, with the shorter days and icier conditions, three to four days is the norm. To maximize our chances of getting up and down the Eiger without unpleasant incident, we figured we needed at least four consecutive days of good weather: one day to allow the buildup of new snow to avalanche off, and three to climb the face and descend the mountain's west flank.

Each morning during our stay at Scheidegg we would crawl out of our tents, plow down through the snowdrifts to the *Bahnhof*, and phone Geneva and Zurich to get a four-day weather forecast. Day after day, the word was the same: Continuing unsettled weather, with rain in the valleys and snow in the mountains. We could do nothing but curse and wait, and the waiting was awful. The Eiger's mythic weight bore down especially hard during the idle days, and it was easy to think too much.

One afternoon, for diversion, we took a ride on the train up to the *Jungfraujoch,* a cog railroad that runs from Kleine Scheidegg to a saddle high on the Eiger-Jungfrau massif. This turned out to be a mistake. The railway traverses the bowels of the Eiger by way of a tunnel that was blasted through the mountain in 1912. Midway up the tracks there is an intermediate station with a series of huge windows that look out from the vertical expanse of the Nordwand.

The view from these windows is so vertiginous that barf bags—the same kind they put in airplane seat-pockets—had been placed on the windowsills. Clouds swirled just beyond the glass. The black rock of the Nordwand, sheathed in frost feathers and sprouting icicles in the places where it overhung, fell away dizzyingly into the mists below. Small avalanches hissed past. If our route turned out to be anything like what we were seeing, we were going to find ourselves in serious trouble. Climbing in such conditions would be desperate if not impossible.

On the Eiger, constructions of the imagination have a way of blurring with reality, and the Eigerwand station was a little too much like a scene from a recurring dream I've been having for years in which I'm fighting for my life in a storm on some endless climb when I come upon a door set into the mountainside. The doorway leads into a warm room with a fireplace and tables of steaming food and a comfortable bed. Usually, in this dream, the door is locked.

A quarter-mile down the tunnel from the big windows of the midway station there is in fact a small wooden door—always unlocked—that opens out onto the Nordwand. The standard route up the wall passes very near this door, and more than one climber has used it to escape from a storm.

Such an escape, however, poses hazards of its own. In 1981, Mugs Stump, one of America's most accomplished alpinists, popped in through the door after a storm forced him to abort a solo attempt on the wall and started walking toward the tunnel entrance, about a mile away. Before he could reach daylight, he met a train coming up the tracks. The guts of the Eiger are hard black limestone that makes for tough tunneling, and when the tunnel was constructed the builders didn't make it any wider than they had to. It quickly became evident to Stump that the space between the cars and the tunnel walls was maybe a foot, give or take a few inches. The Swiss take great pride in making their trains run on time, and it also became evident that this particular engineer was not about to foul up his schedule simply because some damn climber was on the tracks. All Stump could do was suck in his breath, press up against the rock, and try to make his head thin. He survived the train's passing, but the experience was as harrowing as any of the close scrapes he'd had on the outside of the mountain.

DURING OUR THIRD week of waiting for the weather to break, Marc and I rode the train down into Wengen and Lauterbrunnen to find relief from the snow. After a pleasant day of taking in the sights and sipping *Rugenbrau*, we managed to miss the last train up to Scheidegg and were faced with a long walk back to the tents. Marc set out at a blistering pace to try to make camp before dark, but I decided I was in no hurry to get back under the shadow of the Eiger and into the snow zone, and that another beer or two would make the hike easier to endure.

It was dark by the time I left Wengen, but the Oberland trails, through steep (the Swiss, it seems, do not believe in switchbacks) are wide, well maintained, and easy to follow. More important, on this path there were none of the electrified gates that Marc and I had encountered on a rainy night the week before (after missing another train) while walking from Grindelwald to Scheidegg. Such gates are installed to curtail bovine trespassers and are impossible to see in the dark after a few beers. They strike a five-foot nine-inch body at an uncommonly sensi-

tive point precisely six inches below the belt, and with one's feet
clad in soggy Nikes they deliver a jolt of sufficient voltage to
bring forth confessions to crimes not yet committed.

The walk from Wengen went without incident until I neared
the treeline, when I began to hear an intermittent roar that
sounded like someone goosing the throttle of a Boeing 747. The
first gust of wind hit me when I rounded the shoulder of the
Lauberhorn and turned toward Wengernalp. A blast came out
of nowhere and knocked me on my butt. It was the *foehn*, blowing down from the Eiger.

The *foehn* winds of the Bernese Oberland—cousin of the
Santa Ana winds that periodically set Southern California on
fire and the chinooks that roar down out of the Colorado Rockies—can generate stunning power. They are said to hold a dis-
proportionate number of positive ions, and to make people crazy.
"In Switzerland," Joan Didion writes in *Slouching Towards Beth-
lehem*, "the suicide rate goes up during the *foehn*, and in the
courts of some Swiss cantons the wind is considered a mitigating
circumstance for crime." The *foehn* figures prominently in Eiger
lore. It is a dry, relatively warm wind, and as it melts the snow
and ice on the Eiger it brings down terrible avalanches. Typically,
immediately following a *foehnsturm* there will be a sharp freeze,
glazing the wall with treacherous verglas. Many of the disasters
on the Nordwand can be attributed directly to the *foehn;* in *The
Eiger Sanction* it is a *foehn* that almost does Eastwood in.

It was all I could do to handle the *foehn* on the trail through
the cow pastures. I shuddered to think what it would be like to

be hit by one up on the Nordwand. The wind filled my eyes with grit and blew me off my feet over and over again. Several times I simply had to get down on my knees and wait for lulls between gusts. When I finally lurched through the door of the *Bahnhof* at Scheidegg, I found the place packed with railroad workers, cooks, maids, waitresses, and tourists who had become marooned by the storm. The gale raging outside had infected everybody in Scheidegg with some kind of weird, manic energy, and a riotous party was in full swing. In one corner people were dancing to a screaming jukebox, in another they were standing on the tables belting out German drinking songs; everywhere people were calling the waiter for more beer and schnapps.

I was about to join the fun when I spied Marc approaching with a wild look in his eyes. "Jon," he blurted, "the tents are gone!"

"Hey, I don't really want to deal with it right now," I replied, trying to signal the waiter, "Let's just rent beds upstairs tonight and repitch the tents in the morning."

"No, no, you don't understand. They didn't just get knocked down, they fucking blew away. I found the yellow one about fifty yards away from where it had been, but the brown one is gone, man. I looked but I couldn't find it anywhere. It's probably down in Grindelwald by now."

The tents had been tied down to logs, cement blocks, and an ice screw driven securely into frozen turf. There had been at least two hundred pounds of food and gear inside them. It seemed impossible that they could have been carried away by the wind, but they had. The one that was missing had contained our sleeping bags, clothing, my climbing boots, the stove and pots, some food, God only knew what else. If we didn't find it, the weeks of waiting to climb the Nordwand were going to be in vain, so I zipped up my jacket and headed back out into the *foehnsturm*.

By sheer chance I found the tent a quarter-mile from where it had been pitched—drifted over, lying in the middle of the train tracks to Grindelwald. It was a tangled mess of shredded nylon and broken, twisted poles. After wrestling it back to the *Bahnhof*, we discovered that the stove had sprayed butane over everything, and a dozen eggs had coated our clothing and sleeping bags with a nasty, sulphurous slime, but it appeared that no important gear had been lost during the tent's tour of Scheidegg. We threw everything in a corner and returned to the party to celebrate.

The winds at Scheidegg that night were clocked at 170 kilometers per hour. In addition to laying waste to our camp, they knocked down the big telescope on the gift-shop balcony and blew a ski-lift gondola as big as a truck onto the tracks in front of the *Bahnhof*. At midnight, though, the gale petered out. The temperature plummeted, and by morning a foot of fresh powder had replaced the snowpack melted by the *foehn*. Nevertheless, when we called the weather station in Geneva, we were shocked to hear that an extended period of good weather would be arriving in a couple of days. "Sweet Jesus," I thought. "We're actually going to have to go up on the wall."

THE SUNSHINE CAME on October 8, along with a promise from the meteorologists that there would be no precipitation for at least five days. We gave the Nordwand the morning to slough off the post-*foehn* accumulation of snow, then hiked through crotch-deep drifts over to the base of the route, where we set up a hastily patched-together tent. We were in our sleeping bags early, but I was too scared to even pretend to sleep.

At 3 AM, the appointed hour to start up the wall, it was raining and some major ice and rockfall was strafing the face. The climb was off. Secretly relieved, I went back to bed and immediately sank into a deep slumber. I awoke at 9 AM to the sound of birds chirping. The weather had turned perfect once again. Hurriedly, we threw our packs together. As we started up the Nordwand my stomach felt like a dog had been chewing on it all night.

We had been told by friends who had climbed the Nordwand that the first third of the standard route up the face is "way casual." It isn't, at least not under the conditions we found it. Although there were few moves that were technically difficult, the climbing was continuously insecure. A thin crust of ice lay over deep, unstable powder snow. It was easy to see how Ragone had fallen; it felt as though at any moment the snow underfoot was going to collapse. In places where the wall steepened, the snow cover thinned and our ice axes would ricochet off rock a few inches beneath the crust. It was impossible to find anchors of any kind in or under the rotting snow and ice, so for the first two thousand feet of the climb we simply left the ropes in the packs and "soloed" together.

Our packs were cumbersome and threatened to pull us over backward whenever we would lean back to search out the route above. We had made an effort to pare our loads down to the essentials, but Eiger terror had moved us to throw in extra food, fuel, and clothing in case we got pinned down by a storm, and enough climbing hardware to sink a ship. It had been difficult to decide what to take and what to leave behind. Marc eventually elected to bring along a Walkman and his two favorite tapes instead of a sleeping bag, reasoning that when the going got desperate, the peace of mind to be had by listening to the Dead Kennedys and the Angry Samoans would prove more valuable than staying warm at night.

At 4 PM, when we reached the overhanging slab called the Rote Fluh, we were finally able to place some solid anchors, the first ones of the climb. The overhang offered protection from the unidentified falling objects that occasionally hummed past, so we decided to stop and bivouac even though there was more than an hour of daylight left. By digging out a long, narrow platform where the snow slope met the rock, we could lie in relative comfort, head-to-head, with the stove between us.

The next morning we got up at three and were away from our little ledge an hour before dawn, climbing up by headlamp. A rope-length beyond the bivouac, Marc started leading up a pitch that had a difficulty rating of 5.4. Marc is a 5.12 climber, so I was alarmed when he began to mutter and his progress came to a halt. He tried moving left, and then right, but an eggshell-thin layer of crumbly ice over the vertical rock obscured whatever holds there might have been. Agonizingly slowly, he balanced his way upward a few inches at a time by hooking his crampon points and the picks of his axes on unseen limestone nubbins underneath the patina of rime. Five times he slipped, but caught himself each time after falling only a few feet.

Two hours passed while Marc thrashed around above me. The sun came up. I grew impatient. "Marc," I yelled, "if you don't want to lead this one, come on down and I'll take a shot at it." The bluff worked: Marc attacked the pitch with renewed determination and was soon over it. When I joined him at his belay stance, though, I was worried. It had taken us nearly three hours to climb eighty feet. There is more than eight thousand feet of climbing on the Nordwand (when all the traversing is taken into consideration), and much of it was going to be a lot harder than those eighty feet.

The next pitch was the infamous Hinterstoisser Traverse, a 140-foot end run around some unclimbable overhangs, and the key to gaining the upper part of the Nordwand. It was first climbed in 1936 by Andreas Hinterstoisser, whose lead across its polished slabs was a brilliant piece of climbing. But above the pitch he and his three companions were caught by a storm and forced to retreat. The storm, however, had glazed the traverse with verglas, and the climbers were unable to reverse its delicate moves. All four men perished. Since that disaster, climbers have always taken pains to leave a rope fixed across the traverse to ensure return passage.

We found the slabs of the Hinterstoisser covered with two inches of ice. Thin though it was, it was solid enough to hold our ice axes if we swung them gently. Additionally, an old, frayed fixed rope emerged intermittently from the glazing. By crabbing gingerly across the ice on our front points and shamelessly grabbing the old rope whenever possible, we got across the traverse without a hitch.

Above the Hinterstoisser, the route went straight up, past landmarks that had been the stuff of my nightmares since I was ten: the Swallow's Nest, the First Icefield, the Ice Hose. The climbing never again got as difficult as the pitch Marc had led just before the Hinterstoisser, but we were seldom able to get in any anchors. A slip by either of us would send us both to the bottom of the wall.

As the day wore on, I could feel my nerves beginning to unravel. At one point, while leading over crusty, crumbly vertical ice on the Ice Hose, I suddenly became overwhelmed by the fact that the only things preventing me from flying off into space were the two thin steep picks sunk half an inch into a medium that resembled the inside of my freezer when it needs to be defrosted. I looked down at the ground more than three thousand feet below and felt dizzy, as if I were about to faint. I had to close my eyes and take a dozen deep breaths before I could resume climbing.

One 165-foot pitch past the Ice Hose brought us to the bottom of the Second Ice Field, a point slightly more than halfway up the wall. Above, the first protected place to spend the night would be the Death Bivouac, the ledge where Max Sedlmayer and Karl Mehringer had expired in a storm during the first attempt on the Nordwand in 1935. Despite its grim name, the

Death Bivouac is probably the safest and most comfortable bivouac site on the face. To get to it, however, we still had to make an eighteen-hundred-foot rising traverse across the Second Ice Field, and then ascend several hundred devious feet more to the top of a buttress called the Flatiron.

It was 1 PM. We had climbed only about fourteen hundred feet in the eight hours since we'd left our bivouac at the Rote Fluh. Even though the Second Ice Field looked easy, the Flatiron beyond it did not, and I had serious doubts that we could make the Death Bivouac—more than two thousand feet away—in the five hours of daylight that remained. If darkness fell before we reached the Death Bivouac, we would be forced to spend the night without a ledge, in a place that would be completely exposed to the avalanches and rocks that spilled down from the most notorious feature on the Nordwand: the ice field called the White Spider.

"Marc," I said, "we should go down."

"What?!" he replied, shocked. "Why?"

I outlined my reasons: our slow pace, the distance to the Death Bivouac, the poor condition the wall was in, the increasing avalanche hazard as the day warmed up. While we talked, small spindrift avalanches showered down over us from the Spider. After fifteen minutes, Marc reluctantly agreed that I was right, and we began our descent.

Wherever we could find anchors, we rappelled; where we couldn't, we down-climbed. At sunset, below a pitch called the Difficult Crack, Marc found a cave for us to bivouac in. By then we were already second-guessing the decision to retreat, and we spent the evening saying little to each other.

At dawn, just after resuming the descent, we heard voices coming from the face below. Two climbers soon appeared, a man and a woman, moving rapidly up the steps we had kicked two days before. It was obvious from their fluid, easy movements that they were both very, very good climbers. The man turned out to be Christophe Profit, a famous French alpinist. He thanked us for kicking all the steps, then the two of them sped off toward the Difficult Crack at an astonishing clip.

A day after we had wimped-out because the face was "out of condition," it appeared as though two French climbers were going to cruise up the climb as if it were a Sunday stroll. I glanced over at Marc and it looked like he was about to burst into tears. At that point we split up and continued the nerve-wracking descent by separate routes.

TWO HOURS LATER I stepped down onto the snow at the foot of the wall. Waves of relief swept over me. The vise that had been squeezing my temples and gut was suddenly gone. By God, I had survived! I sat down in the snow and began to laugh.

Marc was a few hundred yards away, sitting on a rock. When I reached him I saw that he was crying, and not out of joy. In Marc's estimation, simply surviving the Nordwand did not cut it. "Hey," I heard myself telling him, "if the Frogs get up the sucker, we can always go into Wengen and buy more food, and then go for it again." Marc perked up immediately at this suggestion, and before I could retract my words he was sprinting off to the tent to monitor the French climbers' progress through binoculars.

At this point, however, my luck with the Nordwand finally took a turn for the better: Christophe Profit and his partner only got as far as the Rote Fluh, the site of our first bivouac, before a large avalanche shot past and scared them into coming down, too. A day later, before my Eiger luck could turn again, I was on a jet home.

MAOISTS AND LEECHES

JAMAICA KINCAID

The celebrated author of *Annie John* (1985) and *A Small Place* (1988) was born Elaine Potter Richardson on the Caribbean island of Antigua in 1949. She moved to New York in 1965 to work as an *au pair* and later studied photography at the New York School for Social Research. She began writing for *Ingenue* magazine and in 1973 changed her name to Jamaica Kincaid because her family disapproved of her writing. She began working for the *New Yorker* in the 1980s, met its editor, William Shawn, and eventually married his son Allen, a music professor at Bennington College, Vermont. An ardent gardener, in 2005 she traveled with a group of botanists to Nepal to collect seeds in the Himalayas; the following is from *Among Flowers*, her lively account of that expedition, published in 2006.

. . .

OUR WAY NOW, having left the village, was a steep walk up a landscape that had not so long ago collapsed. We had to climb up and then cross over a recently ravaged hillside (in any other place, it would be a mountainside), that had perhaps not too long ago been the result of a landslide. The evidence of landslides was everywhere, as if proving what goes up must come down is necessary. We, and by this I mean Sue, Bleddyn, Dan, and me, expressed irritation at this with varying intensity (Dan and Bleddyn minor, Sue almost minor, me loudly) and then marched on. Two men, dragging long thick trunks of bamboo attached to porters' straps wrapped around their foreheads, passed us as they were going the other way. They seemed to take our presence for granted, as if they knew about us before they saw us, or as if our presence was typical, or as if we did not matter at all. We marched on; by this juncture we were marching—the leisureliness of walking was not possible once we came in contact with the Maoists. When we got to the top, as usual, it was not at the place of destination. What had seemed to us as the top of the mountain was only the place where the avalanche began. The mountain continued up and it was as if the face of the mountain had decided to fall down starting in its middle. We had to go up some more because, for one thing, Cook, who was always ahead of us—he could walk so fast—could not find any water coming out of the mountain. And also we needed to find some level ground on which to cast our tents, forming our little community of the needy, dependent, plant collectors and the Nepalese people, whose support we could not do without. We kept going up, each turn up above seeming to hold the desirable flatness and water too, for how could that not be so when everywhere we looked we could see a milky white and stiffly vertical flowing line of a waterfall. But Cook went flying up and then went flying down to Sunam, and there were consultations. On our way up, past the place where the avalanche began, we met a herdsman, though before that we had met his cows. At first we made way for the cows because we thought we were in the cows' home and perhaps we should be respectful of them. But the cows remained so cowlike, stubborn and potentially dangerous, if you only considered their horns, and in this case *they* seemed to really consider their horns. The herdsman managed them beautifully, guiding them down and away from us, taking them into the steep bush-covered slopes away from the path they were used to traveling, just to keep us calm. I would not have thought about this incident of the herdsman and his cows again but I saw him the night after this and three nights after this again far away, for me, from all these difficulties.

Between the cows and their herdsman and Cook not finding water to cook us supper, we grew irritable. From our place way up above the village, and even from that way up above the place where we had eaten our lunch, we were closed in. The sun was setting somewhere; we could see the light growing dimmer, literally like someone turning the wick of a lamp lower. We, and by that I mean me in particular and especially, began to whimper and even complain. For one thing, from our vantage point, so high above, we could see the porters carrying our baggage and the tents and all our other supplies and necessities, resting at the place where we had eaten our lunch. So if Cook should find a place in which to cast camp, and casting camp always depended on him, we—and we were so important we felt then—could not enjoy camp, for the things that made sitting in camp comfortable were half a day's walk away. What had the porters been doing all day? someone said—meaning, What had they been doing when we were exploring the landscape, looking for things that would grow in our garden, things that would give us pleasure, not only in their growing, but also with the satisfaction with which we could see them growing and remember seeing them alive in their place of origin, a mountainside, a small village, a not easily accessible place in the large (still) world? We were then having many emotions, feelings about everything: The Maoists were right, I felt in particular: life itself was perfectly fair, people had created many injustices; it was the created injustices that led to me being here, dependent on Sherpas, for without this original injustice, I would not be in Nepal and the Sherpas would be doing something not related to me. And then again, the Maoists were wrong, the porters should be fired; they were not being good porters. They should bend to our demands, among which was to make us comfortable when we wanted to be comfortable. We were very used to being comfortable, and in our native societies (Britain, for Bleddyn and Sue; America, for Dan and me) when we were not comfortable, we did our best to rid ourselves of the people who were not making us comfortable. We wished Sunam would fire the porters. But he couldn't even if he wanted to. There were no other porters around.

We were hungry and tired. It really was getting dark. The sun was going away, not setting. We couldn't see it do that, we could only see the light of day growing dimmer. Still, we could see the porters. They were far away. Way below us. The most forward of them were not even near the place where we had come across the fragrant *Convolvulus*. And there was no real place to camp. No doubt I will always remember this evening, for it was the evening where we could not decide where we would stay, among other things. At just about the time some of the porters were traversing the unpleasant landslide, Sunam decided that we would cast our camp at a spot that was the only level site in the area. Cook had found a stream nearby, in any case, and that was always the deciding factor. We were three-quarters of the way up a steep rising of rock covered with some *Taxus* and *Sorbus* and, instantly recognizable to me, barberry and some kind of raspberry *(Rubus)*. We made our way through them and found we were in a field that had growing in it mostly wormwood, some kind of *Artemisia*. What a relief. And then someone pointed out a leech and then another and then another, and we soon realized that we would camp, we would spend the night in a field full of leeches.

Immediately as we entered this area we were attacked by them. At first it was just one or two seen on the ground, then leaping onto our legs. Then we realized they were everywhere, like mosquitoes or flies or any insect that was a bother, but most insects that were a bother were familiar to us. The leech was not something with which we were familiar. And why was it so frightening, so strange? It was just a simple invertebrate, after all. But a leech is a different kind of invertebrate. To see it whirl itself around as it gathers momentum to fling itself dervishlike onto its victim is terrifying; to see the way it burrows into clothing as it tries to get next to a person's warm skin so it can first make a gash that cannot be felt, for it administers an anesthetic as it bites, is terrifying; to see a thin, steady stream of blood running down your arm or your companion's arm is terrifying, for the leech also administers in its bite an anticoagulant. Was it because it was silent, making no noise of any kind that made it so reprehensible, so shudder-making? A *leech*, just the mere words would make us jumpy, cross. When Dan had first told me of this journey, he had mentioned leeches as one of the disturbing things to be encountered. He had also mentioned altitude sickness and deprivations of everyday comforts such as showers, bathrooms, people you loved, but I remembered leeches more than I remembered Maoists, even when I got to Kathmandu and saw the evidence of a civil war, soldiers with submachine guns everywhere. I remember Dan saying that there will be leeches but we will have so much fun. That night above the Arun River, on the opposite side of the Barun River, looking into the Barun Valley, I was not concerned with anything but the leeches. And so when we walked into our campsite and I saw these little one-inch bugs whirling around and then leaping into the air and landing on us, my spine literally stiffened and curled. I could feel it do this, stiffen and then curl. I screamed loudly and silently at the same time. And then I did what everybody else was doing, Sherpa, porter, and fellow botanist, I forged ahead, grimaced, laughed, searched for the parasites, found them, and picked them off and killed them with great effort and satisfaction. Even so, the disdain and unhappiness for spending the night in a field of leeches never went away.

The stoves were lit and Cook began to make us food. There was no room for our dining tent so the table and chairs were set out on a tarpaulin. We had tea and biscuits, nothing could stop this—and how grateful we were for this. Night fell suddenly, as if someone, somewhere, decided to turn out the light because it suited them right then. After being hot all day, suddenly we were cold and wanted very much to put on our warm clothes. But the clothes were way down below. Sunam had gone back down to hurry up the porters who were carrying our suitcases. The laxness of the porters made Dan and Bleddyn annoyed not only because they couldn't change into dry clothes but also because they wanted to review their collections of the day, try to do some cleaning of seeds, and make some entrances into the collection diaries. We were sitting on our chairs in the open air and looking out on the Barun Valley at night in the Himalaya. It was beautiful. But the leeches kept coming at us. Finally we set up a sort of Leech Patrol; each person, the four travelers, looking for leeches in four different directions.

Our luggage still had not arrived and there was much discussion regarding what the porters had been up to all day. And there was no *chang*, a fermented beverage made from millet, or any other kind of alcoholic beverage as far as we could tell, in the Maoist area. We—I, really—felt small, as if I were a toy, inside the bottom of a small bowl looking up at the rim and wondering what was beyond. The person who lived in a small village in Vermont was not lost to me, the person who existed before that was not lost to me. I was sitting six thousand feet or so up on a clearing we had made on the side of a foothill in the Himalaya. Only in the Himalaya would such a height be called a foothill. Everywhere else this height is a mountain. But from where we sat, we were at the bottom—for we could see other risings high above us, from every direction a higher horizon. The moon came up, full and bright. And it looked like another moon, a moon I was not familiar with. Its light was so pure somehow, as if it didn't shine everywhere in the world; it seemed a moon that shone only here, above us. It sailed across the way, the skyway, that is, majestically, seemingly willful, on its own, not concerned with having a place in the rest of any natural scheme. It was a clear night. We sat on the tarpaulin, on the chairs around the table in a circle, huddled toward the middle to see more clearly and readily the leeches. We were looking up at the sky, clear and full of stars, the light from the moon outlining the tops of the higher hills, and they *were* hills when placed in context of the true risings beyond which we could not see.

It must have been near nine o'clock when we had our dinner. I should have been hungry but I wasn't. I felt sick, my stomach hurt, I wanted to throw up. I was served but could not eat. Dan said that perhaps it was the altitude. We were up at about six thousand feet. Dan flossed and brushed his teeth. I did not. I don't know what Sue and Bleddyn did. Dan and I went into our tent. He reminded me to check my shoes and socks for leeches, to check myself for leeches, to check the space around my sleeping bag for leeches. All was clear and then we settled in to have our nightly review of the day's events, which mostly resulted in huge cackling and laughter. We had finished our cackling and laughter and were about to go to sleep when there occurred a huge storm of fierce thunder and big rain—the kind of thunder and rain that made me think it was pretending to be so fierce and then I thought it was the end of the world, we would never leave this place, the storm would so change the world that we would be forced to stay in the leech field in our tents forever. And it reminded me that this was my first question when confronted with the landscape of the Himalaya: Is this real? It is real enough. We heard Bleddyn calling out to us, Dan and me, that we should check our tent window. Dan and I turned on our flashlights and saw an army of leeches trying to penetrate the window, a square made of mesh netting which served as ventilation on the side of our tent. It was horrifying, not only because we were so far away from everything that was familiar to us. All day as we had marched along, taking a new route to escape the Maoists and their demands, which we felt might include our very lives; we had felt endangered, assaulted, scared. In reality it was just about a dozen leeches, but how to explain to a leech that we did not like President Powell? How to tell a Maoist that Powell wasn't even the president? At some point I stopped making a distinction between the Maoists and the leeches, at some point they became indistinguishable to me, but this was only to me. Fortunately I had acquired some DEET, against Dan's advice, that justifiable denounced insecticide, and I always carried it with me. I reached into my day pack, which was at the foot of my sleeping bag, and sprayed it furiously on the leeches trying to get into our tent and they just fell away and I hoped they were dead. I could not sleep. I wanted desperately to pee but when I thought of the leeches leaping up and then burrowing themselves in my pubic hair, I decided to hold it in. But I couldn't fall asleep and so I went out of our tent, just outside the entrance, and took a long piss. This was a violation of some kind: you cannot take a long piss just outside your tent; you are not to make your traveling companions aware of the actual workings of your body. Not to allow anyone an awareness of the workings of your body is easy to do in our normal lives, where we have access to our own bathrooms, thirty-minute showers of water at a temperature that pleases us, toilets that allow their contents to disappear so completely that to ask where to could be made to seem a case of mental illness. After I had my pee, I took another sleeping pill and went to sleep and did not dream about Maoists, leeches, or anything else. And then I was awakened by a terrifying sound of land falling down from a great height, an avalanche. It sounded quite close by. The morning didn't come soon enough. We got dressed rapidly (I did not brush my teeth), packed up, ate, checked ourselves for leeches, and left. We never wanted to see that place again.

ACKNOWLEDGMENTS

"The First Ascent of the Matterhorn" excerpted from *Scrambles Amongst the Alps in the Years 1860–1869* by Edward Whymper (Washington, D.C.: National Geographic Society, 2002).

"Sunset on Mont Blanc" excerpted from *The Playground of Europe* by Sir Leslie Stephen (Oxford: Basil Blackwell Ltd., 1936).

"Mount Shasta" excerpted from *Picturesque California* by John Muir (San Francisco: J. Dewing and Company, 1888).

"The Holiness of Mountains" excerpted from *Memories, Dreams and Reflections* by C.G. Jung, edited by Aniela Jaffe, translated by Richard & Clara Winston, copyright © 1961, 1962, 1963 and renewed 1989, 1990, 1991 by Random House Inc. Used by permission of Pantheon Books, a division of Random House, Inc.

OTHER TITLES

FROM THE DAVID SUZUKI FOUNDATION
AND GREYSTONE BOOKS

———

Northern Wild by David R. Boyd, ed.

Greenhouse by Gale E. Christianson

Vanishing Halo by Daniel Gawthrop

The Sacred Balance: Rediscovering Our Place in Nature
by David Suzuki and Amanda McConnell

Dead Reckoning by Terry Glavin

Delgamuukw by Stan Persky

The Plundered Seas by Michael Berrill

DAVID SUZUKI FOUNDATION CHILDREN'S TITLES

Salmon Forest by David Suzuki and Sarah Ellis;
illustrated by Sheena Lott

You Are the Earth by David Suzuki and Kathy Vanderlinden

Eco-Fun by David Suzuki and Kathy Vanderlinden

The David Suzuki Foundation works through science and education to protect the diversity of nature and our quality of life, now and for the future.

With a goal of achieving sustainability within a generation, the Foundation collaborates with scientists, business and industry, academia, government and non-governmental organizations. We seek the best research to provide innovative solutions that will help build a clean, competitive economy that does not threaten the natural services that support all life.

The Foundation is a federally registered independent charity, which is supported with the help of over 50,000 individual donors across Canada and around the world.

We invite you to become a member. For more information on how you can support our work, please contact us:

The David Suzuki Foundation
219–2211 West 4th Avenue
Vancouver, BC
Canada v6k 4s2
www.davidsuzuki.org
contact@davidsuzuki.org
Tel: 604-732-4228 · Fax: 604-732-0752

Checks can be made payable to The David Suzuki Foundation. All donations are tax-deductible.
Canadian charitable registration: (BN) 12775 6716 rr0001
U.S. charitable registration: #94-3204049